D0792754

THE SPIRIT OF

SACRIFICE

&

COMMITMENT

EXPERIENCES OF

SEVENTH-DAY ADVENTIST

PIONEERS

COMPILED BY James R. Nix

EDITED BY Fylvia Fowler Kline

Stewardship Department
General Conference of Seventh-day Adventists
Silver Spring, Maryland 20904

Pacific Press Publishing Association
Nampa, Idaho 83687

The Spirit of Sacrifice & Commitment
Copyright 2000 by Stewardship Department, General Conference of
Seventh-day Adventists

Cover design by Tami Pohle
Interior design by Fylvia Fowler Kline and Maureen Hudgins

Most of the content of this book is taken from previously published
work. A complete list of references can be found in the back of the
book. The compiler assumes full responsibility for the accuracy of all
facts and quotations cited in this book.

All rights reserved. No portion of this book may be reproduced in
any form, except for brief excerpts in reviews, without the written
permission of the publishers.

ISBN#   0-9677171-0-8

Published by
Stewardship Department
General Conference of Seventh-day Adventists
Silver Spring, MD 20904

Printed in the U.S.A.
by Pacific Press Publishing Association
Nampa, Idaho

To my friend, teacher, and mentor,
Dr. C. Mervyn Maxwell,
who was the first to challenge me
to share the faith, sacrifice, and commitment
of our Adventist pioneers.
— James R. Nix

Contents

I write not these things to shame the wealthy believer, who is burying himself up in his wealth and his cares, and losing his interest in the cause, and his hold on Heaven; but I design to state facts that you may be led to seek that spirit of sacrifice, which those who were first in this cause evinced, that you may walk in that humble path of obedience in which they walked, and enjoy the blessing of entire consecration, which then rested upon them.
— **James White,** *Life Incidents,* **1868, p. 270.**

Section I

THE MILLERITE ADVENTIST MOVEMENT

1831-1844

1

William Miller

Overpowered by an inward struggle

[A skeptic for several years, William Miller experienced a remarkable conversion in 1816.]

On the Lord's day following [the second anniversary of the Battle of Plattsburg, New York, which had occurred on September 11, 1814, and in which William Miller had participated], it devolved on Captain Miller, as usual in the minister's absence, to read a discourse of the deacons' selection. They had chosen one on the "importance of Parental Duties."[1] Soon after commencing, he was overpowered by the inward struggle of emotion, with which the entire congregation deeply sympathized, and took his seat. His deistical principles seemed an almost insurmountable difficulty with him. Soon after, "Suddenly," he says, "the character of a Saviour was vividly impressed upon my mind. It seemed that there might be a being so good and compassionate as to himself atone for our transgressions, and thereby save us from suffering the penalty of sin. I immediately felt how lovely such a Being must be; and imagined that I could cast myself into the arms of, and trust in the mercy of, such an One. But the question arose, How can it be proved that such a Being does exist? Aside from the Bible, I found that I could get no evidence of the existence of such a Saviour, or even of a future state. I felt that to believe in such a Saviour without evidence would be visionary in the extreme. I saw that the Bible did bring to view just such a Saviour as I needed; and I was perplexed to find how an uninspired book should develop principles so perfectly adapted to the wants of a fallen world. I was constrained to admit that the Scriptures must be a revelation from God. They became my delight; and in Jesus I found a friend. The Saviour became to me the chiefest among ten thousand; and the Scriptures, which before were dark and contradictory, now became the lamp to my feet and light to my path. My mind became settled and satisfied. I found the Lord God to be a Rock in the midst of the ocean of life. The Bible now became my chief study, and I can truly say, I searched it with great delight. I found the half was never told me. I wondered why I had not seen its beauty and glory before, and marvelled that I could have ever rejected it. I found everything revealed that my heart could desire, and a remedy for every disease of the soul. I lost all taste for other reading, and applied my heart to get wisdom from God."

Mr. Miller immediately erected the family altar; publicly professed his faith in that religion which had been food for his mirth,[2] by connecting himself with the little church that he had despised; opened his house for meetings of prayer; and became an ornament and pillar in the church, and an aid to both pastor and people. The die was cast, and he had taken his stand for life as a soldier of the cross, as all who knew him felt assured; and henceforth the badge of discipleship, in the church or world, in his family or closet, indicated whose he was and whom he served.
—**Sylvester Bliss**, *Memoirs of William Miller,* **1853, pp. 66, 67.**

[During the years 1816-1818, Miller was engaged in an intense Bible study. It was then that he discovered the 2300-day prophecy of Daniel 8:14, something with which his name will forever be linked.]

I am a monomaniac

[According to the setting in Sylvester Bliss's Memoirs of William Miller, *this incident happened sometime between 1828 and 1831. However, the following statement that prefaces the same incident suggests it occurred in 1838: "About six years since, the family physician of Mr. Miller had remarked at various places that Esquire Miller was a fine man, and a good neighbor; but on the subject of the advent he was a monomaniac"–*The Midnight Cry*, March 7, 1844, pp. 259, 260. Regardless of the date, the story is worth remembering.]*

As Mr. Miller's opinions respecting the nearness and nature of the millennium became known, they naturally elicited a good deal of comment among his friends and neighbors, and also among those at a distance. Some of their remarks, not the most complimentary to his sanity, would occasionally be repeated to him. Having heard that a physician in his neighborhood had said, "Esquire Miller," as he was familiarly called, "was a fine man and a good neighbor, but was a monomaniac on the subject of the advent," Mr. M[iller] was humorously inclined to let him prescribe for his case.

One of his children being sick one day, he sent for the doctor, who, after prescribing for the child, noticed that Mr. Miller was very mute in one corner, and asked what ailed him.

"Well, I hardly know, doctor. I want you to see what does, and prescribe for me."

The doctor felt his pulse, &c., and could not decide respecting his malady; and inquired what he supposed was his complaint.

"Well," says Mr. Miller, "I don't know but I am a monomaniac; and I want you to examine me, and see if I am; and, if so, cure me. Can you tell when a man is a monomaniac?"

The doctor blushed, and said he thought he could. Mr. Miller wished to know how.

"Why," said the doctor, "a monomaniac is rational on all subjects but one; and, when you touch that particular subject, he will become raving."

"Well," says Mr. Miller, "I insist upon it that you see whether I am in reality a monomaniac; and if I am, you shall prescribe for and cure me. You shall, therefore, sit down with me two hours, while I present the subject of the advent to you, and, if I am a monomaniac, by that time you will discover it."

The doctor was somewhat disconcerted; but Mr. Miller insisted, and told him, as it was to present the state of his mind, he might charge for his time as in regular practice.

The doctor finally consented; and, at Mr. Miller's request, opened the Bible and read from the 8th of Daniel. As he read along, Mr. Miller inquired what the ram denoted, with the other symbols presented. The doctor had read Newton, and applied them to Persia, Greece, and Rome, as Mr. Miller did. Mr. Miller then inquired how long the vision of those empires was to be.

"2300 days."

"What!" said Mr. Miller, "could those great empires cover only 2300 literal days?"

"Why," said the doctor, "those days are years, according to all commentators; and those kingdoms are to continue 2300 years."

Mr. M. then asked him to turn to the 2d of Daniel, and to the 7th; all of which he explained the same as Mr. Miller. He was then asked if he knew when the 2300 days would end. He did not know, as he could not tell when they commenced.

Mr. Miller told him to read the 9th of Daniel. He read down till he came to the 21st verse, when Daniel saw "the man Gabriel," whom he had "seen in the vision."

"In what vision?" Mr. Miller inquired.

"Why," said the doctor, "in the vision of the 8th of Daniel."

"'Wherefore, understand the matter and consider the vision.' He had now come, then, to make him understand that vision, had he?"

"Yes," said the doctor.

"Well, seventy weeks are determined; what are these seventy weeks a part of?"

"Of the 2300 days."

"Then do they begin with the 2300 days?"

"Yes," said the doctor.

"When did they end?"

"In A.D. 33."

"Then how far would the 2300 extend after 33?"

The doctor subtracted 490 from 2300, and replied, 1810. "Why," said he, "that is past."

"But," said Mr. Miller, "there were 1810 from 33; in what year would that come?"

The doctor saw at once that the 33 should be added, and set down 33 and 1810, and, adding them, replied, 1843.

At this unexpected result the doctor settled back in his chair and colored; but immediately took his hat and left the house in a rage.

The next day he again called on Mr. Miller, and looked as though he had been in the greatest mental agony.

"Why, Mr. Miller," said he, "I am going to hell. I have not slept a wink since I was here yesterday. I have looked at the question in every light, and the vision must terminate about A.D. 1843; and I am unprepared, and must go to hell."

Mr. Miller calmed him, and pointed him to the ark of safety; and in about a week, calling each day on Mr. M., he found peace to his soul, and went on his way rejoicing, as *great a monomaniac* as Mr. Miller. He afterwards acknowledged that, till he made the figures 1843, he had no idea of the result to which he was coming.—**ibid., pp. 94-97.**

The solemn covenant

[Miller's decision to start preaching was not made easily. Years later, he recalled the day he decided to start publicly sharing his views about the soon return of Christ.]

The public labors of Mr. Miller, according to the best evidence to be obtained, date from the autumn of 1831. He had continued to be much distressed respecting his duty to "go and tell it to the world," which was constantly impressed on his mind. One Saturday, after breakfast, he sat down at his desk to examine some point, and, as he arose to go out to work, it came home to him with more force than ever, "Go and tell it to the world." He thus writes:—

"The impression was so sudden, and came with such force, that I settled down into my chair, saying, 'I can't go, Lord.' 'Why not?' seemed to be the response; and then all my excuses came up—my want of ability, &c.; but my distress became so great, I entered into a solemn covenant with God, that, if he would open the way, I would go and perform my duty to the world. 'What do you mean by opening the way?' seemed to come to me. 'Why,' said I, 'if I should have an invitation to speak publicly in any place, I will go and tell them what I find in the Bible about the Lord's coming.' Instantly all my burden was gone, and I rejoiced that I should not probably be thus called upon, for I had never had such an invitation. My trials were not known, and I had but little expectation of being invited to any field of labor.

"In about half an hour from this time, before I had left the room, a son of Mr. [Silas] Guilford[3] of Dresden [New York], about sixteen miles[4] from my residence, came in, and said that his father had sent for me, and wished me to go home with him. Supposing that he wished to see me on some business, I asked him what he wanted. He replied, that there was to be no preaching in their church the next day, and his father wished to have me come and talk to the people on the subject of the Lord's coming. I was immediately angry with myself for having made the covenant I had; I rebelled at once against the Lord, and determined not to go. I left the boy, without giving him any answer, and retired in great distress to a grove near by. There I struggled with the Lord for about an hour, endeavoring to release myself from the covenant I had made with him; but I could get no relief. It was impressed upon my conscience, 'Will you make a covenant with God, and

break it so soon?' and the exceeding sinfulness of thus doing overwhelmed me. I finally submitted, and promised the Lord that, if
he would sustain me, I would go, trusting in him to give me grace
and ability to perform all he should require of me. I returned to
the house, and found the boy still waiting. He remained till after
dinner, and I returned with him to Dresden.

"The next day, which as nearly as I can remember, was about
the first Sabbath [Sunday] in August, 1833,[5] I delivered my first
public lecture on the Second Advent. The house was well filled
with an attentive audience. As soon as I commenced speaking, all
my diffidence and embarrassment were gone, and I felt impressed
only with the greatness of the subject, which, by the providence of
God, I was enabled to present. At the close of the services on the
Sabbath, I was requested to remain and lecture during the week,
with which I complied. They flocked in from the neighboring
towns; a revival commenced, and it was said that in thirteen families all but two persons were hopefully converted.

"On the Monday following I returned home, and found a
letter from Elder [Isaac] Fuller, of Poultney, Vt., requesting me to
go and lecture there on the same subject. They had not heard of
my going to Dresden. I went to Poultney, and lectured there with
similar effect.

"From thence I went, by invitation, to Pawlet, and other towns
in that vicinity. The churches of Congregationalists, Baptists, and
Methodists, were thrown open. In almost every place I visited my
labors resulted in the reclaiming of backsliders, and the conversion of
sinners. I was usually invited to fields of labor by the
ministers of the several congregations whom I visited, who gave me
their countenance; and I have never labored in any place to which I
was not previously invited. The most pressing invitations from the
ministry, and the leading members of the churches, poured in continually from that time, during the whole period of my
public labors, and with more than one half of which I was unable to
comply. Churches were thrown open everywhere, and I lectured, to
crowded houses, through the western part of Vermont, the northern

part of New York, and in Canada East; and powerful reformations were the results of my labors." —**ibid., pp. 97-99.**

Stagecoaches and dollars

[Miller's motivation to travel and preach was not honorariums, per diem, or mileage reimbursement! Rather, his was a self-supporting ministry.]

During this tour, while in Canada [between June 21 and July 9, 1835], a woman placed two half-dollars in his hand, which was all the assistance he received previous to 1836. His expenses for travel, &c., were paid from his own funds.—**ibid., pp. 122, 123.**

On the 19th of June [1836] he visited Lansingburgh, N.Y., and continued till the 26th. To pay his stage-fare he received, on this occasion, four dollars, which, with the two half-dollars received in Canada, was all the remuneration he had thus far received for his expenses. Subsequent to that time, as he says in his [1845] "Apology and Defence," he never received enough to meet his expenses of travel to the places where he was invited; so that his public labors were never of any pecuniary advantage to him, as has been currently reported and believed; but, on the contrary, they were a heavy tax on his property, which gradually decreased during that period of his life.—**ibid., p. 125.**

[The date of the letter as printed in Bliss is mistakenly given as February 4, 1844.]

"As to worldly cares, I have had but very few for twelve years past. I have a wife and eight children; I have great reason to believe they all are the children of God, and believers in the same doctrine with myself. I own a small farm in Low Hampton, N.Y.; my family support themselves upon it, and I believe they are esteemed frugal, temperate and industrious. They use hospitality without grudging, and never turn a pilgrim from the house, nor the needy from the door. I bless God my family are benevolent and kind to all men who need their sympathy or aid; I have no cares to manage, except my own individual wants; I have no funds or debts due me of any amount; 'I owe no man any thing;" [sic.]

and I have expended more than two thousand dollars of my property in twelve years, besides what God has given me through the dear friends, in this cause."—**Portion of a letter printed in the *Signs of the Times* from William Miller to Joshua V. Himes, written from Philadelphia, February 4, 1843; ibid., p. 181.**

Notify the world

[Although the Millerites, as Miller's followers came to be known, were eventually expelled from the churches to which they had belonged, Miller had no desire to establish his own church. Converting souls and helping people prepare for Christ's soon return was his sole motivation for preaching.]

"In all my labors I never had the desire or thought to establish any separate interest from that of existing denominations, or to benefit one at the expense of another. I thought to benefit all. Supposing that all Christians would rejoice in the prospect of Christ's coming, and that those who could not see as I did would not love any the less those who should embrace this doctrine, I did not conceive there would ever be any necessity for separate meetings. My whole object was a desire to convert souls to God, to notify the world of a coming judgment, and to induce my fellowmen to make that preparation of heart which will enable them to met their God in peace. The great majority of those who were converted under my labors united with the various existing churches."—**From William Miller, *Apology and Defence*, 1845; ibid., p. 328.**

No visions or fancies of his own

[At the invitation of Elder Timothy Cole, whom he had never met, William Miller lectured in Lowell, Massachusetts, May 14-22, 1838. The story of Miller's arrival in Lowell, his initial reception by Elder Cole, and Cole's subsequent conversion to Millerism illustrates the impact Miller's preaching had, not just on congregations, but also on pastors.]

Previous to Mr. Miller's visit to Massachusetts, Elder T[imothy] Cole, of Lowell, had heard of the results attending his labors in Vermont, and had written for him to visit that city. The dress of Mr. Miller was very plain and ordinary, much more befitting his profession of a farmer than of a preacher. Elder Cole, from the reports of his great success, expected him to appear like some distinguished doctor of divinity. When Mr. M. came to Randolph, Elder C. obtained a promise of his services in Lowell, to commence on the 14th of May, and was requested to meet him at the cars. He had heard that Mr. Miller wore a camlet cloak and white hat, but expected to see a fashionably-dressed gentleman. On the arrival of the cars, he went to the depot to meet him. He watched closely the appearance of all the passengers as they left the cars, but saw no one who corresponded with his expectations of Mr. M. Soon he saw an old man, shaking with the palsy, with a white hat and camlet cloak, alight from the cars. Fearing that this one might prove to be the man, and if so, regretting that he had invited him to lecture in *his* church, he stepped up to him, and whispered in his ear,—

"Is your name Miller?"

Mr. M. nodded assent.

"Well," said he, "follow me."

He led the way, walking on ahead, and Mr. M. keeping as near as he could, till he reached his house. He was much chagrined that he had written for a man of Mr. M.'s appearance, who, he concluded, could know nothing respecting the Bible, but would confine his discourse to visions and fancies of his own.

After tea, he told Mr. M. he supposed it was about time to attend church; and again led the way, Mr. M. bringing up the rear. He showed Mr. M. into the desk, but took a seat himself among the congregation. Mr. M. read a hymn; after it was sung he prayed, and read another hymn, which was also sung. He felt unpleasant at being left in the pulpit alone, but took for his text: "Looking for that blessed hope, and the glorious appearing of the great God and our Saviour Jesus Christ."[6] This he sustained and illustrated by apposite quotations of Scripture, proving a second personal and glorious appearing of Christ. Elder C. listened for about fifteen minutes, when, seeing that he presented nothing but the word of God, and that he opened the Scriptures in a manner that did honor to the occasion, like a workman who needeth not to be ashamed, he walked up into the pulpit, and took his seat. Mr. M. lectured there from the 14th to the 22d of May, and again from the 29th to the 4th of June. A glorious revival followed, and Elder C. embraced his views in full, continuing for six years a devoted advocate of them.—**ibid., pp. 135, 136.**

The courteous preacher

[Miller visited Portland, Maine, on two occasions: March, 1840, and June, 1842. On both occasions Ellen Harmon (later White), along with her family, attended Miller's series of lectures. Years later, she recalled the impact that Miller's sincerity had on his hearers. As a result of attending these meetings, Ellen and her family became Millerite Adventists.]

Mr. Miller's manner of preaching was not flowery or oratorical, but he dealt in plain and startling facts, that roused his hearers from their careless indifference. He supported his statements and theories by Scripture proof as he progressed. A convincing power attended his words, that seemed to stamp them as the language of truth.

He was courteous and sympathetic. When every seat in the house was full, and the platform and places about the pulpit seemed overcrowded, I have seen him leave the desk, and walk down the aisle, and take some feeble old man or woman by the hand and find a seat for them, then return and resume his discourse. He was indeed rightly called "Father Miller," for he had a watchful care over those who came under his ministrations, was affectionate in his manner, of a genial disposition and tender heart.—**Ellen G. White, *Life Sketches*, 1915, p. 27.**

To Him be all the glory

I call heaven and yourselves to witness, my brethren, that I have never taught any thing to make you throw away any part of God's word. I have never pretended to preach any thing but the Bible. I have used no sophistry.

My preaching has not been with words of man's wisdom. I have not countenanced fanaticism in any form. I use no dreams or visions except those in the word of God. I have taught you no precept of man, nor the creed of any sect. I have never designed to make a new sect, or to give you a *nick name;* this the enemies of Christ's second advent have done—and we must patiently bear it until he comes, and then he will take away our reproach. I have wronged no man, neither have I sought for your honors or gold. I have preached about 4,500 lectures in about twelve years, to at least 500,000 different people. I have broken my constitution and lost my health—and for what? That if possible I might be the means of saving some. How many have been saved by these means I cannot tell—God knows—to him be all the glory. In one thing I have great reason to rejoice. I believe I have never lectured in any place, but God has been with me and given me some fruits of his Spirit, as an evident token of the truth. I have never preached or believed in any time for Christ to come but the end of the prophetic periods, which I have always believed would end with the Jewish year 1843; and which I still believe, and mean, with the help of God, to look for until he comes. And I think I can say with my whole heart and soul,—Amen, even so come, Lord Jesus. **—Portion of an address given by William Miller at the Millerite Conference held in New York City, February 6-9, 1844; as printed in *The Midnight Cry*, February 15, 1844, p. 236.**

Scoffers must scoff

[Miller's reaction to all the derision of him after the first disappointment in the Spring of 1844, when Christ did not come as expected, is a powerful testimony to any today who are tempted to complain about the difficulties of being an Adventist. At the time, Miller was the object of public ridicule in many American newspapers; the butt of jokes told about him and his followers; and the recipient of scorn heaped upon him by an overwhelmingly skeptical public and clergy.]

On April 5 [1844] Miller wrote to Elon Galusha that he was "looking every day and hour for Christ to come." He looked forward to being "like him, whom twenty-eight years ago I loved . . . . I thought before this time I should be with him, yet I am here a pilgrim and a stranger, waiting for a change from mortal to immortal."

Miller went on to note that the scoffers must scoff, but, he affirmed, God would take care of him. "Why then," he queried, "should I complain if God should give a few days or even months more as probation time, for some to find salvation, and others to fill up the measure of their cup, before they drink the dregs, and wring them out in bitter anguish. It is my Savior[']s will and I rejoice that he will do things right.—**Letter written by William Miller to Elon Galusha, April 5, 1844, quoted in George Knight, *Millennial Fever*, 1993, p. 162.**

Twice disappointed, but not discouraged

[Miller's reaction to the "passing of the time" on October 22, 1844, as described in a letter written on November 10, 1844, to Joshua V. Himes, demonstrates his unshakable faith in God despite his disappointment in Christ not having returned as expected.]

Although I have been twice disappointed, I am not yet cast down or discouraged. God has been with me in spirit, and has comforted me. I have now much more evidence that I do believe in God's word. My mind is perfectly calm, and my hope in the coming of Christ is as strong as ever . . . .

Brethren, hold fast, let no man take your crown. I have fixed my mind on another time, and here I mean to stand until God gives me more light, and that is, *to-day, to-day,* and *to-day,* until he comes.—**Portion of a letter written by William Miller to Joshua V. Himes, quoted in Bliss, *William Miller,* pp. 277, 278.**

Shouting in death

[Miller's unshakable confidence in Christ's soon return continued right up to the time of his death on December 20, 1849. During the last few months of his life, he was confined to his bed. When his death appeared to be imminent, a telegram was sent to his close friend and associate, Joshua V. Himes, to come to Low Hampton, New York. Himes arrived on December 17, 1849. Although virtually blind and very feeble, Miller recognized his friend and colleague. One of the few things Miller said to Himes was the following.]

"Tell them (the brethren) we are right. The coming of the

Lord draweth nigh; but they must be patient, and wait for him."
—William Miller; quoted in Bliss, *William Miller*, p. 377.

[Miller's death came three days later.]

The closing scene finally came. On the 20th of December
[1849], in the morning, it was manifest to all that he must soon
depart. During the morning he made no particular conversation,
but would break forth in expressions like the following: "Mighty
to save!" "O, I long to be there!" "Victory! victory!" "Shouting in
death!" &c.

He finally sunk down into an easy sleeping or dozing state.
Occasionally he roused up, and opened his eyes, but was not able
to speak, though perfectly rational, and knew us all. He continued
to breathe shorter and shorter, till five minutes past three o'clock,
P. M., when he calmly and sweetly gave his last breath.**—ibid.,
p. 378.**

Tumbling to the dust

*[The following are the closing lines from a letter William Miller wrote on March
26, 1832, to Truman Hendrix, a Baptist minister who was among the first to
accept Miller's views. It demonstrates how vivid the second coming of Christ was
in Miller's thinking, even years before 1844.]*

Look!—look again! See crowns, and kings, and kingdoms
tumbling to the dust! See lords and nobles, captains and mighty
men, all arming for the bloody, demon fight! . . . See,—see these
signs!

Behold, the heavens grow black with clouds; the sun has veiled
himself; the moon, pale and forsaken, hangs in middle air; the hail
descends; the seven thunders utter loud their voices; the light-
nings send their vivid gleams of sulphurous flame abroad; and the
great city of the nations falls to rise no more forever and forever!
At this dread moment, look! look!—O, look and see! What means
that ray of light? The clouds have burst asunder; the heavens
appear; the great white throne is in sight! Amazement fills the
universe with awe! He comes!—he comes! Behold, the Saviour

comes! Lift up your heads, ye saints,—he comes! he comes!—he comes!

"Wm. Miller"

—Closing of William Miller's letter to Truman Hendrix, March 26, 1832; ibid., p. 102.

2
Joseph Bates

Preaching in a tavern

[Early in 1844, Joseph Bates sold his home in Fairhaven, Massachusetts, to pay for his preaching activities which included a trip to Maryland, a destination against which he had been warned.]

About this time I sold my place of residence,[7] including the greater portion of my real estate, paid up all my debts, so that I could say once more that I owed "no man anything." For some time I had been looking and waiting for an open way to go down South into the slaveholding States with the message. I was aware that slave holders in the South were rejecting the doctrine of the second advent, and but a few months before had ordered Brn. Storrs and Brown from the city of Norfolk, Virginia, and I was told that if I went South the slaveholders would kill me for being an abolitionist. I saw there was some danger, but imperative duty and a desire to benefit them and unburden my own soul, overbalanced all such obstacles.

Bro. H. S. Gurney,[8] now living in Memphis, Mich., said he would accompany me as far as Philadelphia. . . . [There] we attended some of the crowded meetings of Bro. Miller and others. It was truly wonderful to see the multitudes of people gathered to hear him preach the coming of the Lord. Bro. G. now concluded to accompany me South. We reached the city of Annapolis, Maryland, by the way of Washington, and crossed the Chesapeake Bay through the ice to the central part of Kent Island, on which I had been cast away some twenty-seven winters before. At the tavern we found the people assembled for town meeting. The trustees of two meeting-houses who were present, were unwilling to open their doors for us, and intimated the danger of preaching the doctrine of Christ's coming among the slaves. We applied to the tavern-keeper for his house; he replied that we could have it as soon as the town meeting closed.

We then made an appointment before them, that preaching on the second advent would commence in the tavern the next afternoon at a given hour. Said the keeper of the tavern, "Is your name Joseph Bates?" I answered, "Yes." He said that he remembered my visiting his father's house when he was a small boy, and informed me that his mother and family were in another room and would be glad to see me. His mother said she thought she knew me when I first came to the house.

The notice of our meeting soon spread over the island, and the people came to hear, and soon became deeply interested about the coming of the Lord. Our meetings continued here, I think, for five successive afternoons. The mud was so deep, on account of a sudden thaw, that we held no evening meetings. The tavern was a temperance house, and accommodated us much better than any other place we could have found in the vicinity.

At the commencement of our last afternoon meeting, a brother who had become deeply interested in the cause, called Bro. G. and myself aside to inform us that there was a company about two miles off at a rum store, preparing to come and take us. We assured him that we were not much troubled about it, and urged him to go into the meeting with us and leave the matter in their hands. The people seemed so earnest to hear that my anxiety increased to make the subject as clear as I could for them, so that the ideas of being taken from the meeting had entirely passed from me. But before I had time to sit down, a man who was at the meeting for the first time, whom I knew to be a Methodist class-leader, and one of the trustees that refused us the use of their meeting-house, arose and commenced denouncing the doctrine of the Advent in a violent manner, saying, that he could destroy or put down the whole of it in ten minutes. I remained standing, and replied, "We will hear you." In a few moments he seemed to be lost in his arguments, and began to talk about *riding us on a rail.* I said, "We are all ready for that, sir. If you will put a saddle on it, we would rather ride than walk." This caused such a sensation in the meeting that the man seemed to be at a loss to know which way to look for his friends.

I then said to him, "You must not think that we have come six hundred miles through the ice and snow, at our own expense, to give you the Midnight Cry, without first sitting down and count-ing the cost. And now, if the Lord has no more for us to do, we had as lief lie at the bottom of the Chesapeake Bay as anywhere else until the Lord comes. But if he has any more work for us to do, you can't touch us!"

One Dr. Harper arose and said, "Kent, you know better! This man has been giving us the truth, and reading it out of the Bible, and I believe it!" In a few minutes more Mr. Kent shook me heart-ily by the hand and said, "Bates, come and see us!" I thanked him, and said my work was so pressing I did not think I should have time; but I would come if I could. But we had no time to visit only those who had become deeply interested, and wished us to meet with them in their praying circles. At the close of our meeting we stated that we had the means, and were prepared to defray all the expenses of the meeting cheerfully, unless some of them wished to share with us. They decided that they would defray the expenses of the meeting, and not allow us to pay one cent.—**Joseph Bates,** *Autobiography of Joseph Bates,* **1868, pp. 277-280.**

3

Charles Fitch[9]

Believing till death

The cause of his death, in October, 1844, was a fever which was brought on in the following way. He had a large number of new believers who desired baptism, and others who had not yet made up their minds. The company who were ready went with him to the lake, and there were baptized. A cold wind was blowing as he, with them, started in his wet garments for home, and he was much chilled. But he had not gone far when he met another company from among those whom he had left behind, who now came desiring baptism. He went back with them to the lake and also immersed them. Then as they started home there came a third company whose conviction of sin and of Jesus' salvation and of His soon coming had brought them to the decision. At their request he turned again and baptized them also. The next day, though ill from the effects of his chill, he rode in the cold wind some miles to another appointment. This proved too hard on him, and he was stricken down, and after an illness of several weeks he died.[10] His last clear words, in answer to some who asked him of his faith, were, "I believe in the promises of God."—**Arthur W. Spalding, *Pioneer Stories of the Second Advent Message*, 1922, pp. 99, 100.**

Faith celebrated in obituary

This dear brother has fallen asleep in Jesus. Those lips from which the words of God have been poured forth with power upon so many thousands of listening ears, are now sealed. That heart, which beat with a father's tenderness, and a brother's love for the children of God, has ceased beating.

After his arduous labors at Morrisville and St. Georges' camp-meetings, he left New York for Cleveland, on Monday, September 16. At Rochester, while apparently in perfect health, he stated, in a public meeting that he had a presentiment that he must sleep a little while before the coming of the Lord. On arriving at Buffalo, he was attacked with a severe bilious fever, and died on Monday, October 14th, in full faith that he should awake in a few days in the likeness of his Redeemer. Bro. Williamson, who passed through Buffalo on his return from the West, wrote to us Oct. 17th: "I saw his remains yesterday. Sister Fitch is there, without a tear, expecting to meet her husband very soon. So far from sorrow, she is smiling and happy."

Brother Fitch embraced the doctrine of the Advent when its friends were few, and [as] early as 1838. In 1841, he took a decided stand on this question, and gave to the public his reasons for embracing it, in a letter to Bro. [Josiah] Litch. Since then he has been laboring heart and soul in the spread of this truth. He has been an efficient instrument of good, and his labors have been blessed to the conversion of many souls. He was formerly the pastor of the Fourth Congregational church in Hartford, Ct.; from which he removed his relation in 1836, to the church at the Marlboro' Chapel, of Boston. After that he preached awhile in Newark, N.J.; and also in Haverhill, Mass. There he came out boldly in the cause of the Advent, and cast his all upon the issue.

He has left a widow and family of children, who mourn not as those without hope. "Blessed are the dead which die in the Lord from henceforth. Yea, saith the Spirit, that they may rest from their labors, and their works do follow them.' [sic.]

His widow and fatherless children are now at Cleveland, confidently expecting the coming of our Lord to gather the scattered members of the family.—**"Brother Charles Fitch,"** *The Midnight Cry*, **October 31, 1844, p. 142.**

4

Leonard Hastings

As in the day of Noah

[Leonard and Elvira Hastings, of New Ipswich, New Hampshire, previously Miller-
ites, were among the earliest Sabbath keepers. Leonard Hastings wrote this letter
to his church asking that his membership be discontinued because of his belief in
the soon return of Christ.]

To the Orthodox Congregational Church at New Ipswich, N.
H. Sept. 17, 1843

Believing as I do that the Second Advent of the Lord in 1843
is plainly and clearly taught in the gospel and also that Christian
perfection or sanctification is required of us in God's Word and
that in and through the atonement of the Lord Jesus there is ample
provision made for our sanctification and full redemption in this
world and knowing as I do that as a church you do regret and
make light of these glorious truths and even say that men may go
on sinning to Heaven and also that Christ cannot come in the clouds
of Heaven these thousand years, I therefore feel it my duty in
compliance with what God says by John the Revelator, "Come

out of her my people that ye be not partakers of her sins and that ye receive not of her plagues," do request of you that my name be erased from the church record as I shall no longer consider myself a member of your church. I feel that I do this in conformity to the requirements of the Great Head of the church, and now in His name I beseech you all not to make light any more of the coming of the blessed Lord for at the appointed time He will come and will not tarry; all the unbelief of the world will not stop Him, so do get ready by making a full consecration of yourselves to the living God, for as in the day of Noah so shall the coming of the Son of Man be.

Yours in the belief of the coming of Christ in 1843.

Leonard Hastings

—Leonard Hastings' original letter is preserved in the Heritage Room, Loma Linda University Library, Loma Linda, California.

5

Joshua V. Himes

Going where doors are opened

[Miller gave his first series of lectures in Boston December 8-16, 1839, in the Chardon-Street Chapel, where Himes pastored. It was at this time that Himes converted to Millerism and decided to join Miller in preaching the soon return of Christ.]

At this time he [Miller] stopped at the house of Elder Himes, who had much conversation with him respecting his views, his plans for the future, and his responsibilities. Elder H. became impressed with the correctness of Mr. M's views respecting the nearness and nature of Christ's coming; but was not fully satisfied respecting the time. He was, however, sufficiently convinced that Mr. Miller was communicating important truths, to feel a great interest in their promulgation.

"When Mr. Miller had closed his lectures," says Elder H., "I found myself in a new position. I could not believe or preach as I had done. Light on this subject was blazing on my conscience day and night. A long conversation with Mr. Miller then took place, on our duties and responsibilities. I said to Bro. Miller, 'Do you really believe this doctrine?'

"He replied, 'Certainly I do, or I would not preach it.'

"'What are you doing to spread or diffuse it through the world?'

"'I have done, and am still doing, all I can.'

"'Well, the whole thing is kept in a corner yet. There is but little knowledge on the subject, after all you have done. If Christ is to come in a few years, as you believe, no time should be lost in giving the church and world warning, in thunder-tones, to arouse them to prepare.'

"'I know it, I know it, Bro. Himes,' said he; 'but what can an old farmer do? I was never used to public speaking: I stand quite alone; and, though I have labored much, and seen many converted to God and the truth, yet *no one,* as yet, seems to enter into the *object* and *spirit of my mission,* so as to render me much aid. They like to have me preach, and build up their churches; and there it ends, with most of the ministers, as yet. I have been looking for help,—I want help.'

"It was at this time that I laid myself, family, society, reputation, all, upon the altar of God, to help him, to the extent of my power, to the end. I then inquired of him what parts of the country he had visited, and whether he had visited any of our principal cities.

"He informed me of his labors,"—as given in the foregoing pages.[11]

"'But why, 'I said, 'have you not been into the large cities?'

"He replied that his role was to visit those places where invited, and that he had not been invited into any of the large cities.

"'Well,' said I, 'will you go with me where doors are opened?'

"'Yes, I am ready to go anywhere, and labor to the extent of my ability to the end.'

"I then told him he might prepare for the campaign; for doors should be opened in every city in the Union, and the warning should go to the ends of the earth! Here I began to 'help' Father Miller." —Bliss, *William Miller,* **pp. 139-141.**

May my last days be peaceful and useful

[Although Himes never accepted the seventh-day Sabbath, and for years opposed the work of Seventh-day Adventists, he never lost faith in the soon, literal return of Christ. In his old age Himes suffered from cancer, and came to the Battle Creek Sanitarium for treatments. While a patient there, he wrote to Ellen G. White, who was then living and working in Australia.]

At 90, my general health is good and I will soon return to my people,[12] for work as usual, in hope of good fruit. I hope my last days may be peaceful and useful as well. I preach the Advent as being near, without a definite time, and I believe it . . . .

You and your associates have done a great work since 1844— and still go on. I do not know what is to be the end of it . . . . I finished my work really, in 1844, with Father Miller. After that, what I have done at most was to give comfort to the scattered flock . . . . I will soon go to my rest. You are younger and may work on. God bless and guide you to the end. I enclose five dollars for YOUR OWN USE.—**Letter from Joshua V. Himes to Ellen G. White, September 12, 1894; quoted in Paul A. Gordon,** *Herald of the Midnight Cry,* **1990, p. 117.**

Now in relation to your work I am no judge, you are to judge of that, and do it as best you can. Father Miller's work with mine as a helper, was done faithfully . . . . The day of the Lord will reveal the result.—**Letter from Joshua V. Himes letter to Ellen G. White, March 13, 1895; ibid., p. 117**.

[Ellen White responded to Himes' donation in letters written to him and to "Sister Austin," a friend of Himes.]

The spirited participation evidenced by your donation for this field has rejoiced my heart; for it testifies that you have not lost the missionary spirit which prompted you first to give yourself to the work, and then to give your means to the Lord to proclaim the first and second angels' messages in their time and order to the world. This is a great gratification to me; for it bears an honorable testimony that your heart is still in the work.—**Ellen G. White, Letter 31a, 1895, to Joshua V. Himes; ibid., p. 118.**

I have written a short letter to Elder J. V. Himes. I cannot express to you my joy at the evidence that one of the pioneers in the work of giving the message of warning to the world in 1840-44 is acting a part in giving the third angel's message . . . . To me this is a great satisfaction. I know that we have the truth, and one who had so decided a part to act in the proclamation of the first and second angels' messages, is highly esteemed by me for his works' sake. This donation for Australia is gladly received from Elder Himes; it is more precious in my estimation than it would be if coming from any other human agent.—**Ellen G. White, Letter 1a, 1895 to Sister Austin; ibid., pp. 117, 118**

6

James White

Neither horse, saddle, bridle, nor money

In October, 1842, an Advent camp-meeting was held in Exeter, Me., which I attended. The meeting was large, tents numerous, preaching clear and powerful, and the singing of Second-Advent melodies possessed a power such as I had never before witnessed in sacred songs. My Second-Advent experience was greatly deepened at this meeting, and at its close I felt that I must immediately go out into the great harvest-field, and do what I could in sounding the warning. I therefore prepared three lectures, one to remove such objections as the time of the advent not to be known, and the temporal millennium, one on the signs of the times, and one on the prophecy of Daniel.

I had neither horse, saddle, bridle, nor money, yet felt that I must go. I had used my past winter's earnings in necessary clothing, in attending Second-Advent meetings, and in the purchase of books and the chart. But my father offered me the use of a horse for the winter, and Elder Polley gave me a saddle with both pads torn off, and several pieces of an old bridle. I gladly accepted these, and cheerfully placed the saddle on a beech log and nailed on the pads, fastened the pieces of the bridle together with malleable nails, folded my chart, with a few pamphlets on the subject of the advent, over my breast, snugly buttoned up in my coat, and left my father's house [in Palmyra, Maine] on horseback.— **White, *Life Incidents*, pp. 72, 73.**

A 22-year-old and a broken-down horse

On a January morning, in 1843, James White mounted his horse and rode away on a preaching tour among total strangers, his light clothing giving him scant protection from the cold . . . .

On April 2 [1843] James headed for home. The snow on the road was still very deep. Often he had to dismount and plunge into the drifts to relieve the horse as it struggled through the piled-up snow.

On the fifth of April, James White rode his poor broken-down horse into the yard of his home in Palmyra. He had been gone for four [three] months. It was later reported at the next [Christian Connection] church conference that during those four [three] months a thousand souls had joined the church as a result of the work of 22-year-old James White!

A few days after his arrival in Palmyra, James White was ordained as a minister of the Christian [Connection] Church.—**Virgil Robinson, *James White*, 1976, pp. 23, 26.**

7

Camp Meeting at Exeter, New Hampshire

Upon the wings of the wind

[Bates traveled North, from where he was living in Fairhaven, Massachusetts, to attend what turned out to be an extremely important Millerite camp meeting. It was at this camp meeting that Samuel S. Snow riveted his audience's attention by pointing them to the Fall of 1844 as being the precise time for fulfilling the antitypical ancient Jewish Day of Atonement at the end of the 2300-day prophecy of Daniel 8:14.]

On the 12th of August,[13] another [camp meeting] was held in Exeter, N. H. On my way there [by train], something like the following seemed to be continually forcing upon my mind. "You are going to have new light here, something that will give a new impetus to this work . . . ."

There was light given and received there, sure enough; and when that meeting closed, the granite hills of New Hampshire rang with the mighty cry, *Behold the Bridegroom cometh; go ye out to meet him!* As the stages and railroad cars rolled away through the different States, cities, and villages of New England, the rumbling of the cry was still distinctly heard. Behold the bridegroom cometh! Christ is coming on the tenth day of the seventh month! Time is short, get ready! get ready. . . ! ! Who does not still remember how this message flew as it were upon the wings of the wind—men and women moving on all the cardinal points of the compass, going with all the speed of locomotives, in steamboats and rail cars, freighted with bundles of books and papers, wherever they went distributing them almost as profusely as the flying leaves of autumn.—**Joseph Bates, *Second Advent Way Marks and High Heaps*, 1847, pp. 30, 31.**

Breaking down before God

[James White, who was living at home with his parents in Palmyra, Maine, when not out preaching, also attended the historic New Hampshire camp meeting.]

Language cannot describe the solemnity of that hour . . . . The time for shouting, and display of talent in speaking, singing, and praying, seemed to be past. The brethren and sisters calmly consecrated themselves and their all to the Lord and His cause, and with humble prayers and tears sought his pardon and his favor.—**White, *Life Incidents*, p. 166.**

[The following is James White's description of another camp meeting held a short time later in Maine, in what he and the others believed to be earth's waning hours.]

Sins were confessed with tears, and there was a general breaking down before God, and strong pleadings for pardon, and a fitness to meet the Lord at his coming . . . . Before that meeting closed, hundreds testified with tears of joy that they had sought the Lord and found Him, and had tasted the sweets of sins forgiven.

The parting was most solemn. That was the last camp-meeting the brethren expected to attend on these mortal shores. And as brother shook the hand of brother, each pointed the other to the final gathering on the immortal shores at the grand encampment of the saints in the new Jerusalem. Tears flowed profusely, and strong men wept aloud. —**ibid., pp. 167, 168.**

8

Preparing for the "Great Disappointment"

A calm mind and pleasurable expectation

The time immediately preceding the 22nd of October was one of great calmness of mind and pleasurable expectation on the part of those who regarded that point of time with interest. There was a nearness of approach to God, and a sweetness of communion with him, to which those who experienced it will ever recur with pleasure. During the last ten days, secular business was, for the most part, suspended: and those who looked for the Advent gave themselves to the work of preparation for that event, as they would for death, were they on a bed of sickness, expecting soon to close their eyes on earthly scenes forever.—**Bliss, *William Miller*, pp. 275, 276.**

Adventism prevailed and reigned

All grew more enthusiastic. Crops were left unharvested, their owners expecting never to want what they had raised. Men paid up their debts. Many sold their property to help others pay their debts, who could not have done it themselves. Beef cattle were slaughtered and distributed among the poor. At no time since "the day of pentecost was fully come" had there been the like—a day when that Pentecost was so completely duplicated as in 1844, When Adventism prevailed and reigned.—**Luther Boutelle**, *Sketch of the Life and Religious Experience of Elder Luther Boutelle*, **1891, p. 63.**

Such a concentration of thought; such a oneness of faith was never before witnessed; certainly not in modern times. All that did speak spoke the same things. Solemn, yet joyful. Jesus coming! we to meet him! [sic.] Meetings everywhere were being held. Confessions made, wrongs righted; sinners inquiring what they should do to be saved. Those who were not with us were mightily effected. Some were exceedingly frightened with awful forebodings.—**ibid., p. 67.**

Searching of heart, confession of sin

I think I have never seen among our brethren such *faith* as is manifested in the seventh month. "He will come," is the common expression. "He will not tarry the second time," is their general reply. There is a forsaking of the world, an unconcern for the wants of life, a general searching of heart, confession of sin, and a deep feeling in prayer for Christ to come. A preparation of heart to meet him seems to be the labor of their agonizing spirits. There is something in this present waking up different from anything I have ever before seen. There is no great expression of joy: that is, as it were, suppressed for a future occasion, when all heaven and earth will rejoice together with joy unspeakable and full of glory. There is no shouting; that, too, is reserved for the shout from heaven. The singers are silent: they are waiting to join the angelic hosts, the choir from heaven. No arguments are used or needed: all seem convinced that they have the truth. There is no clashing of sentiments: all are of one heart and of one mind. Our meetings are all occupied with prayer, and exhortation to love and obedience. The general expression is, "Behold, the Bridegroom cometh; go ye out to meet him." Amen. Even so come, Lord Jesus!

"William Miller"

—Letter written by William Miller on October 11, 1844; quoted in Bliss, *William Miller*, pp. 270, 271.

More necessary than food and drink

With diligent searching of heart and humble confessions we came prayerfully up to the time of expectation. Every morning we felt that it was our first work to secure the evidence that our lives were right before God. Our interest for one another increased; we prayed much with and for one another. We assembled in the orchards and groves to commune with God and to offer up our petitions to Him, feeling more fully in His presence when surrounded by His natural works. The joys of salvation were more necessary to us than our food and drink. If clouds obscured our minds, we dared not rest or sleep till they were swept away by the consciousness of our acceptance with the Lord.—**Ellen G. White,** *Testimonies for the Church,* **vol. 1, 1885, p. 55.**

9

Millerite Faith in Action

Money will do me no good

I had some things for sale; when any person came to buy, I would let them have these articles. When they wanted to pay for them I would not receive it, telling them that the world was coming to an end by such a time, and I needed no money as it would do me no good. Of course they sometimes stared at me, astonished.—**Henry B. Bear, *Henry B. Bear's Advent Experience*, date unknown, p. 3.**

Potatoes survive winter's wrath

Silas Guilford, William Miller's brother-in-law, . . . had moved from Dresden to near Oswego, New York. There he and his boys, on their farm, planted a twelve-acre field of potatoes in the spring of 1844. It will be recalled that Adventists had their first disappointment over the Lord's not coming in April of 1844. Then came the "tarrying time." At first they set no other date; and so, seeing nothing certainly in the future, they planted their spring crops. But during the summer came the "midnight cry," with October 22 set as the day of the Advent. Thus it occurred that Adventists, without denying their faith, planted their crops, but some at least would not harvest them.

Guilford and his family put every dollar they could get into the cause of the Second Advent, and he mortgaged his farm, and put in that money too. He also left his potatoes in the ground that fall, that they might preach his faith in the Lord's coming. The snows came early in his section, and covered them up, so they stayed over the winter. When it came spring, and the snow was gone, Silas Guilford said to his wife, "I'm going up to the potato field and see if there are any potatoes that are good."

"Oh, don't, Silas," said his wife. "You've been ridiculed so much. And now if they see you up there trying to dig potatoes, it will be just too much."

"Well," he said, "the boys and I are going up anyway." Irving [Erving], the oldest boy, told this to [Elder James] Shultz when the latter was a lad.

"I went up with father," he said. "The ground was thawed out nicely. Father put his fork in. The first hill he dug up—wonderfully nice potatoes! He felt of them; they were solid, not frozen at all, and not a bit of rot. The next hill too! And then he sent me racing back for the other boys, and we dug those whole twelve acres—a fine yield. We got $4.50 a bushel for them, enough to pay off the mortgage and leave a tidy sum."—**Arthur W. Spalding,** ***Footprints of the Pioneers***, **1947, pp. 71,72.**

No potato rot here

The Lord recognizes sacrifices made for his name's sake, as will be seen in the case of those who left crops unharvested to show their faith in his near appearing. I will cite one instance, which will serve to illustrate the providences that favored many others. Brother Hastings, of New Ipswich, N.H., had a large field of splendid potatoes which he left undug. His neighbors were anxious about them, and came to him offering to dig them and put them in the cellar for him *free,* if he would let them, "for" said they, "you may want them." "No!" said Brother Hastings, "I am going to let that field of potatoes preach my faith in the Lord's soon appearing."

That fall, as may be learned from the Claremont (N. H.) *Eagle,* the New York *True Sun,* and various other public journals, the potato crop was almost a total loss from the "potato rot." As expressed in the *Sun,* "How painful it is to learn that whole crops of this valuable esculent have been destroyed by the rot. A correspondent of a Philadelphia paper says the potato crop in that State is ruined. The only section from which little complaint is heard, is Maine, but even there the crop has not escaped the disease."

As the fall was mild, and Brother Hastings's potatoes were left in the ground until November, none of them rotted. Consequently he had an abundant supply for himself and his unfortunate neighbors who had been so solicitous for his welfare the previous October, and who, in the spring, were obliged to buy seed potatoes of him, and were glad to get them by paying a good price. What they had supposed was going to be such a calamity to Brother Hastings, God turned to a temporal blessing, not only to him, but to his neighbors also.—**John N. Loughborough,** *Rise and Progress of the Seventh-day Adventists,* **1892, pp. 85, 86.**

In honor of the King of kings

MILLERISM. I. T. Hough, tailor and draper, Fifth street, below Market, Philadelphia, has closed his store, and placed the following inscription on his shutters:

> This shop is closed in honor
> of the King of Kings,
> Who will appear about the
> 22d of October.
> Get ready, friends, to crown
> him Lord of all.

—Brief news note appearing in the *Portland Tribune,* **Portland, Maine, October 12, 1844, p. 214 [p. 6], col. 4.**

Section II

EARLY SABBATH-KEEPING
ADVENTISM
1845-1849

1

Acceptance of the Seventh-day Sabbath

No other day but the one God gave

[Three teenagers: Marian Stowell (1829-1913), Oswald Stowell (1828-1918), and J. N. Andrews (1829-1883), were among the very first of the former Millerites to accept the seventh-day Sabbath in 1845.]

In the spring of 1845 one of Elder [T. M.] Preble's tracts was sent to my father,[14] containing extracts from reliable historians telling how the Sabbath—the seventh day of the week—had merged into Sunday observance, with no claim of divine authority for the change. All references to the Bible were hunted out, that were given in this to me wonderful tract. The promise made was fresh in my memory. I expected to stand alone. From my heart I said, "No other day but the one God gave and sanctified will I observe."

I handed the tract to my older brother,[15] saying nothing. He was ready to join me. It was Friday; he split up all the wood necessary for over Sunday. I made my usual loaf of cake that I might not be a Sabbath-breaker any longer.

The next Monday I gave the tract to J. N. Andrews. He read and returned it, saying, "Have your father and mother read this?"

"No, but I have, and found that we are not keeping the right Sabbath. Are you willing to keep the right Sabbath, Brother John?"

"Indeed I am, Will you keep it with me, M_____?"

"Of course, Brother O. and I kept last Sabbath. We will be glad to have you join us; but you take Elder Preble's tract back for your father and mother to read without saying one word in regard to it."

"All right."

Very soon came the words, "Have Brother and Sister Stowell read this tract?"

"No," was their son's reply, "but M. and O. have."

One room soon held us all. Two families kept the next "Lord's day," not the first day of the week, but the one given to our first parents in their Eden home.

There was missionary work to be done, and no time to lose. My father enclosed a ten-dollar bill in a letter, directed as follows: "To a Seventh-day Baptist Minister, Hopkinton, R. I." Soon after came Father Griswald, as we called him, bringing with him the ten-dollar package my father had ordered.

Elder G. was surprised to find us followers of William Miller, and still strong believers in his doctrine after the disappointment. The distribution of these Seventh-day Baptist tracts soon added to our small number seven other families, representing North and South Paris, Norway, and Woodstock, Me. Soon after an excellent tract came from the pen of Elder Joseph Bates, the reading of which brought in our beloved Elder James White and his wife.— **Mrs. M. C. Stowell Crawford, "A Letter from a Veteran Worker,"** ***The Watchman*, April 25, 1905, p. 278.**

Praise God for the clear light

[Once fully convicted of the seventh-day Sabbath, nothing could stop Joseph Bates from observing it or from sharing it with others. In time, Bates came to be known in Adventist history as "The Apostle of the Sabbath."]

My friends and neighbors, and especially my family, know that I have for more than twenty years strictly endeavored to keep the first day of the week for the Sabbath, and I can say that I did it in all good conscience before God, on the ocean, and in foreign countries as well as my own, until about sixteen months since I read an article in the Hope of Israel, by a worthy brother, T. M. Preble, of Nashua [New Hampshire], which when I read and compared with the bible [sic.], convinced me that there never had been any change. Therefore the seventh day was the Sabbath, and God required me as well as him to keep it holy. Many things now troubled my mind as to how I could make this great change, family, friends, and brethren and, but this one passage of scripture was, and always will be as clear as a sunbeam. *"What is that to thee: follow thou me."* In a few days my mind was made up to begin to keep the fourth commandment, and I bless God for the clear light he has shed upon my mind in answer to prayer and a thorough examination of the scriptures on this great subject. Contrary views did, after a little, shake my position some, but I feel now that there is no argument nor sophistry that can becloud my mind again this side of the gates of the Holy City.—**Joseph Bates, *The Seventh- Day Sabbath, A Perpetual Sign, From the Beginning to the Entering into the Gates of the Holy City, According to the Commandment*, 1846, p. 40.**

Prudence Bates was a devoted wife. She had approved of her husband's spending his money in the cause of the coming of Christ, for she held with him in that. But . . . she was not with him in this new Sabbath truth, nor was she for yet four years. During that time he used to drive with her to her Christian church on Sunday, go home, and come back to get her after service, for he would not keep the pope's sabbath; he kept the Lord's Sabbath. In 1850 she followed him into the third angel's message, with its Sabbath truth, and for twenty years, until her death, she was a devoted and beautiful Sabbathkeeping Christian worker.[16]—**Spalding**, *Footprints of the Pioneers*, p. 47.

2

The First Publications

Poor in cash and rich in faith

[Although not a Sabbath-keeping paper, <u>The Day-Star</u> was the first publication that carried what eventually developed into our sanctuary doctrine. The article contained the results of the combined study of O. R. L. Crosier, Dr. F. B. Hahn, and Hiram Edson. Among others, Edson helped put up the money to print this "Extra" section, which was featured on the last page of the newspaper.]

To the Brethren and Sisters Scattered Abroad

We have prayerfully examined the subject presented by Brother [O. R. L.] Crosier[17] in the light of God's word, and are fully satisfied it is meat in due season, and if properly examined and understood will settle many difficulties in the minds of many brethren at this time.

In order to get it before the brethren, it becomes necessary to loan the money necessary for its publication, with the expectation that all who feel interested and have means will aid in the expense. The expense as near as we can now ascertain will be about $30. Brethren here, as in most other places, are poor, (but rich in faith) but we can bear one-half of the expense, and will more if necessary.

If more should be refunded than the other half, it will be sent to Bro. [Enoch] Jacobs, or as brethren may direct. The subject, brethren, is now before you, and we do pray you will examine it carefully by the Word. May the Lord add his blessing.

The brethren will please direct to F. B. Hahn,[18] Canandaigua, Ont. Co., N.Y.

HIRAM   EDSON.

F. B. HAHN.

—Hiram Edson and F. B. Hahn, *The Day-Star* "Extra," February 7, 1846, p. 44.

[Hiram and Esther Edson's daughter later recalled her mother's involvement in defraying the cost of The Day-Star *"Extra"]*

After the passing of the time when they expected the Lord would come, the 22d of October, 1844, a few of the most earnest and faithful ones were at the home of my father (Hiram Edson) praying and studying the prophecies to learn the cause of the disappointment. After prayer they started out to visit some who had been interested, and were going through a cornfield, when suddenly father saw a bright light shining around him and heard these words, as if spoken by an audible voice: "The temple of God was opened in heaven, and there was seen in his temple the ark of his testimony."

The others passed on, but soon noticed that he was not with them, and looking back, asked what was the matter. He replied, "Brethren, there is new light for us."

They began to study the prophecies, and the light on the subject of the sanctuary came to them, which fully explained the cause of the disappointment. O. R. L. Crosier then wrote the article mentioned in the REVIEW a few months ago. He was at my father's, and finances being low and those interested in the message having used all their ready means in proclaiming the message, my mother[19] sold her solid silver teaspoons and half of her large spoons to pay for having the article printed in the *Day Dawn*.[20] That also opened up the subject of the seventh-day Sabbath.—**Mrs. V. O. Cross, "Recollections of the Message,"** *The Advent Review and Sabbath Herald*, **April 1, 1920, p. 22.**

Vision in print

[The first separate publication of Ellen G. Harmon (later White) was a broadside entitled "To the Little Remnant Scattered Abroad." It was dated April 6, 1846. Half the printing expenses was borne by Heman S. Gurney[21] of Fairhaven, Massachusetts.]

Word came to us one day that a woman was to speak in the Advent hall in New Bedford [Massachusetts]. She was to relate a vision, etc. I went to hear her. The vision was the same as has since been published as Sr. White's first vision. I could see no reason to find fault with her appearance or what she said. She appeared like a humble, conscientious Christian. I learned her name and address, but was slow to advocate her course. Fanaticism was appearing in some places, and I wished to prove all things, and hold fast that which was good. I found she was creating some sensation where she met the little company to relate, as she said, what God had shown to her. I thought, If this is something the remnant must meet, I must know where it came from. I therefore went to Portland, Me., and inquired for Mr. Harmon[22] (the father of this young lady). I found the family living in a humble cottage. I introduced myself, and was made welcome after telling them I had come to make their acquaintance, especially the acquaintance of sister Ellen Harmon. I found them a humble, devoted, God-fearing family. I visited a number of places where she was known, and all testified to her devoted, self-sacrificing character. I spent a number of weeks with the family and in their vicinity, and became convinced that the fountain was good, and that God had called sister Harmon to an important work. I found a brother[23] who was willing to pay one half of the expense of printing her first vision. We arranged with the printer, and I left for home.—**H. S. Gurney, "Recollections of Early Advent Experience,"** *Review and Herald*, **January 3, 1888, p. 2.**

The vision "To the Remnant" was given soon after the disappointment in 1844. A small edition of about 250 copies was printed in Portland, Maine, on a foolscap sheet, and circulated among the few believers and honest ones. The last page of the sheet was left partly blank so that those receiving this document could have a place to write out their opinions of the same, whether favorable or unfavorable, and return to the publisher if they wished. Elder James White was the publisher and Bro H. S. Gurney, now of Memphis, Mich., stood half of the expense of printing. This was the <u>first</u> form in which any of the views of Mrs. E. G. White were published.[24] This was in the spring of 1846.—**H. S. Gurney, "Gurney Statement Re 'To the Remnant,'" May 15, 1891.**

In the spring of 1845 I became a Seventh-day Adventist.[25] A small company of Adventist believers came out about the same time, embracing the Sabbath and contending for the original advent faith as held in 1844. We were waiting for further light on the prophecies. About this time Sister White (as I shall call her; her name was Harmon—married to Brother White a few years after this) came to New Bedford, Mass. to relate what the Lord had shown her in vision. A few from Fairhaven went over the river— one mile[26]—to hear what she had to say; her delivery was free and clear, altho only 16 years old[27]. Her sister Sarah[28] was older, who always traveled with her for company and defense. I did not then get acquainted with her, but determined in my mind to know the family she came from. A few days from this found me in Portland, Me. at the house of Brother Harmon—found the whole family firm Seventh-day Adventists, consecrated, devoted Christian people. I stopped with them and in the vicinity several weeks and became well acquainted with all their work, which was chiefly to visit the little bands who were holding fast their confidence and faith in the '44 movement, and trying to strengthen, encourage, and correct. I visited some of the little companies with her and found her an earnest, devoted, consistent laborer. . . . I returned to Portland prepared to leave for home, but first I arranged with Brother White to get Sister White's first vision printed, and I would pay one-half the expense. From this point onward I never have doubted that Sister White's work and visions have a very close connection with the third angel's message.—**H. S. Gurney, "Early Day Experiences Recounted by H. S. Gurney," typescript copy of statement written by Gurney to his son C. H. Gurney, April 12, 1896.**

The anonymous benefactor

[In August, 1846, Joseph Bates published his first pamphlet advocating the seventh-day Sabbath. The 48-page pamphlet, entitled "The Seventh Day Sabbath, A Perpetual Sign, From the Beginning, to the Entering into the Gates of the Holy City, According to the Commandment," cited biblical reasons that convinced James and Ellen White to accept the Sabbath shortly after their marriage on August 30, 1846.]

The work and payment on the book went on until the day the book was to be completed and delivered. There was a balance due on the book. Heman Gurney, an unmarried man who was a blacksmith, decided to leave his employer, and go with Brother Bates as a singing evangelist.[29] When he went to his employer and notified him that he was going to leave, and called for the hundred dollars due him, the man refused to pay, and said, "Your thus suddenly leaving me is more than one hundred dollars' damage to my business."

But later, on the morning the books were to be delivered, Brother Gurney's old employer met him on the street and said, "Gurney, I honestly owe you one hundred dollars, and here it is," handing him the money. Brother Gurney said to himself, "The Lord is in this. I will go at once and pay the balance due on Brother Bates' books."

When Brother Bates called later in the day to excuse the matter of delay in payment, the printer said, "A man came in early this morning and paid the balance due. I know not his name. He was a stranger to me."

Brother Gurney told me of this after Brother Bates' death. That faithful servant of the Lord never knew, to the day of his death, who paid the balance on the books. So his books, by God's providence, were not delayed a day.—**J. N. Loughborough, "Second Advent Experience-No. 4,"** *Review and Herald,* **June 28, 1923, pp. 9, 10.**

"Father held a note against a man from whom he had never been able to collect, and this note had become outlawed and legally worthless, and he never expected to realize anything from it. But one day while on the street, this man, seeing father, called to him, and said: 'I want to pay my note,' which he did. Father, believing that the Lord had sent this man to him with the money, at once went to the printer, and paid the entire bill for the printing of the tract referred to;[30] and he did not tell Brother Bates he had done this, nor did Brother Bates ever know who paid the bill. The man in the print shop did not know father, for he did not reveal his identity."—**Charles H. Gurney, letter to H. E. Rogers, January 24, 1940.**

A shilling, a wife, and a barrel of flour

[The famous "York Shilling" story has sometimes been associated with the publication of Joseph Bates' first small tract on the Sabbath. However, based on the following two sources, it seems more likely that the story actually pertained to the publication of Bates' later 116-page publication entitled A Vindication of the Seventh-day Sabbath, and the Commandments of God: With a Further History of God's Peculiar People, From 1847 to 1848. *The preface in this small book is dated January, 1848.]*

In the autumn of 1847, Bro. Bates sat down to write a work of more than one hundred pages, with only a York shilling at his command.—**James White,** *Life Incidents,* **1868, p. 269.**

Brother Bates . . . is in the work of God. Just before he came to Bristol Conference was asked by his wife to get her some flour for she had only part enough to make a loaf of bread. Brother Bates had only money enough to buy two pounds of flour so off he went and soon he came in with two pounds of flour. His wife asked, what have you been doing? What will you do next? She declared that she would not bake it. Brother Bates is in the work of God. His last work was right in the main. . . .

My best love to all the faithful. Pray for us. Brother Bates said he would send you the Sabbath tracts. You have received them I expect. Ellen will write soon I expect.—**James White letter to "My Dear Brother" [Stockbridge Howland], July 2, 1848.**

Elder Joseph Bates, of Fairhaven, Mass. . . . accepted the Sabbath in 1845, and at once began to preach the truth from State to State. He soon saw that a book, or even a tract, on the Sabbath question would be a great help to him in his work, and his soul was moved by the Spirit of God to write and publish something on this subject. But how it could be done without money, was the question, as all he had was a York shilling (twelve and a half cents). It may be of interest to the reader to relate his experience in this matter just as he told it to me in 1855.

He said that while in prayer before God, he decided to write the book, and felt assured that the way would open to publish it. He therefore seated himself at his desk, with Bible and concordance, to begin his work. In the course of an hour, Mrs. Bates came into the room and said, "Joseph, I haven't flour enough to make out the baking;" and at the same time mentioned some other little articles that she needed. "How much flour do you lack?" asked Captain Bates. "About four pounds," was her reply. "Very well," replied he. After she left the room, he went to a store near by, purchased the four pounds of flour and the other articles, brought them home, and again seated himself at his writing desk. Presently Mrs. Bates came in and saw the articles on the table and exclaimed, "Where did this flour come from?" "Why," said the Captain, "isn't there enough? you said you wanted four pounds." "Yes," said she, "but where did you get it?" "I bought it," said he; "is not that the amount you wanted to complete the baking?" "Yes," continued Mrs. Bates, "but have *you*, Captain Bates, a man who has sailed vessels out of New Bedford to all parts of the world, been out and bought *four* pounds of flour?" "Yes, was not that the amount you needed to complete the baking?" "Yes," said Mrs. Bates, "but have you bought *four pounds* (!) of flour?"

Another trial soon followed. When Captain Bates left the sea, he sold out his interest in a ship for $11,000, but now he had spent his all to advance the cause of truth. Up to this date Mrs. Bates did not know his true financial condition, but he felt that he must now acquaint her with it, so he calmly said, "Wife, I spent for those articles the last money I have on earth." With bitter sobs Mrs. Bates inquired, "What are we going to do?" The Captain arose, and with all the dignity of a captain directing his vessel, said, "I am going to write a book; I am going to circulate it, and spread this Sabbath truth before the world." "Well," said Mrs. Bates, through blinding tears, "what are we going to live on?" "The Lord is going to open the way," was Captain Bates's smiling reply. "Yes," said Mrs. Bates, "the Lord is going to open the way! that's what you always say," and bursting into tears she left the room.

After Captain Bates had continued his work for half an hour, the impression came to him to go to the post-office, as there was a letter there for him. He went, and sure enough there was a letter. In those days the postage on letters was five cents, and prepayment was optional. The writer of this letter had for some reason failed to pay the postage. And here again the Captain was humbled, as he was obliged to tell the postmaster, Mr. Drew, with whom he was well acquainted, that he could not pay the postage, as he had no money; but he said, "Will you let me see where it is from?" "Take it along," said the postmaster, "and pay some other time." "No," said the Captain, "I will not take the letter out of the office until the postage is paid."

While he had the letter in his hand, he said, "I am of the opinion that there is money in this letter," and turning to the postmaster, he asked, "Will you please open it? If there is money in it, you can take the postage out; if not, I will not read it." The postmaster complied with his request, and lo! it contained a ten-dollar bill. He found, by reading, that the letter was from a person who said the Lord so impressed his mind that Elder Bates was in need of money that he hastened it to him; and in the haste he probably forgot to pay the postage.

After paying the postage he went to a provision store, bought a barrel of flour for $4, besides potatoes, sugar, and other necessary articles. When giving orders where they were to be delivered, he said, "Probably the woman will say they don't belong there, but don't you pay any attention to what she says; unload the goods on the front porch." He then went to the printing-office[31] and made arrangements for publishing one thousand copies of a tract of about one hundred pages, with the understanding that as the copy was furnished the printers[32] were to put it in type as rapidly as possible, sending proofs to him. He was to pay for the work as fast as he received the money, and the books were not to be taken from the office until the bills were all paid. Captain Bates knew well there was no money due him, but he felt it his duty to write this book, believing that the Lord would move on hearts to send the money when it was needed. After purchasing paper, pens, etc., thus giving time for the household supplies to go in advance of him, he went to the head of the street leading to his house. On seeing that the articles were there, he went into the house by the back entrance, and seated himself again at his desk. Mrs. Bates came in and said excitedly, "Joseph, just look out on the front porch. Where did that stuff come from? A drayman came here and would unload it. I told him it didn't belong here, but he would unload it." "Well," said Captain Bates, "I guess it's all right." "But," said Mrs. Bates, "where did it come from?" "Well," said the Captain, "the Lord sent it." "Yes," said Mrs. Bates, "the Lord sent it! that's what you always say." He then handed the letter to his wife, saying, "Read this, and you will know where it came from." She read it, and again retired for another cry, but it was of a different character from the first; and on returning she humbly asked his pardon for her lack of faith.—**Loughborough,** *Seventh-day Adventists,* **pp. 110-113.**

3

The Indefatigable "Captain Bates"³³

A housekeeper's purse and heart

Those who up to this time (1847) had accepted the third angel's message, were poor in this world's goods, and consequently could do but little financially for the spread of the message. Elder White and his wife and Elder Bates saw the importance of personal labor among the scattered brethren, and also the necessity of preparing reading matter to place in the hands of the people, as an aid in leading them to the knowledge of the truth. Elder Bates was aided much in presenting the Sabbath question by his tract on that subject, as he went to different localities, and by the circulation of the same through the mail. He labored with the utmost perseverance. At one time, owing to a lack of money with which to pay his fare, he was about to start on foot to go from Massachusetts to New Hampshire. Just then he received a letter from a young sister who had engaged to do house-work at $1 per week that she might have something with which to help the cause. After working one week, she was so impressed with the thought that Elder Bates needed money that she went to her employer and obtained advanced pay so as to enable her to send him at once $5. With this he paid his fare to New Hampshire, by public conveyance. At every place he had good meetings, and many souls accepted the truth.—**Loughborough,** *Seventh-day Adventists,* **pp. 132, 133.**

I well remember when Bro. Bates felt deeply impressed with the duty to labor in Vermont, and, being destitute of means, resolved to start on foot from Fairhaven, Mass. A natural sister[34] of Mrs. W. had come from Maine to Fairhaven, to perform the duties of the kitchen for one dollar a week, and in this way raise means to spread the truth. On learning Bro. Bates' intention to perform the long journey on foot, she went to her employer and asked for five dollars, which she obtained and gave to Bro. Bates to help him on his way to Vermont. God greatly blessed the mission, as many witnesses, who still observe the Sabbath, can testify.—**White,** *Life Incidents,* **p. 270.**

Ticketless travel

On another occasion Captain Bates was under conviction to go to a certain place, and actually took his seat in the train, having neither money nor ticket. He had been in his seat only a few moments when a man who was a perfect stranger to him came and handed him $5 to assist him in his work. Such providences were common in the life of this devoted pioneer, and he was always so sure of the divine help just when it was needed that he was never known to hold back from any enterprise that promised to help forward the cause he loved.—**M. Ellsworth Olsen,** *Origin and Progress of Seventh-day Adventists,* **1925, p. 188.**

Wading through snow

Dear Bro. White: Since I started, in Oct. last, on my western tour, I have visited many places in western N.Y. Held protracted meetings in several places with our Sabbath brethren, who are loving the present truth more and more. In many places we found the brethren in deep trials; but prayer, and perseverance in the strait [sic] truths that the little flock, now see in their pathway soon triumphed over the Enemy, and our hearts were made glad and healed by the precious saving truths in the third angel's message.

Bro. [Hiram] Edson met me at Auburn N.Y. We crossed the St. Lawrence, for Canada West,[35] the last week in Nov., and have been working our way to the west, along the south shore of Lake Ontario, and wherever we have learned that there were scattered sheep in the back settlements north of us, we have waded through the deep snow from two to forty miles to find them, and give the present truth; so that in five weeks we have traveled hundreds of miles, and gained on the direct road westward one hundred eighty miles, We expect to close our labors here by the 5th, and then go north again to Lake Sincoe [sic], where we learn there are some of the scattered flock. From thence it is probable we shall pass on the same course westward to the borders of Lake Huron and Erie. When we have finished our labors between these seas, we expect to return towards Rochester, N.Y.

The first twenty days of our journey we were much tried with the deep snow, and tedious cold weather, and with but few exceptions cold and impenetrable hearts. The truth was no food for them. Since that time the scene has changed and the truth begun to take effect, and some we trust are now searching for the truth. —**Joseph Bates**, *Review and Herald*, **January 13, 1852, p. 80.**

4

Sacrifice and the Sabbath Conference

Jesus fared no better

My husband went through the streets of Brunswick, [Maine], with a bag upon his shoulder in which were a few beans and a little meal and rice and flour to keep us from starvation. When he entered the house singing, "I am a pilgrim and I am a stranger," I said, Has it come to this?

Has God forgotten us? Are we reduced to this? He lifted his hand and said, "Hush, the Lord has not forsaken us. He gives us enough for our present wants. Jesus fared no better." I was so worn that as he said this, I fainted from the chair. The next day a letter came asking us to go to another conference. We had no money. When my husband went to the post office for his mail, he found a letter containing five dollars. When he returned he gathered the family together and offered a prayer of thanksgiving. This is the way the work began.

At one time light came that we should go to Portsmouth [New

Hampshire]. But we had no money. We got all ready and were waiting when a man came riding very fast to our door. Jumping from his wagon, he said, There is somebody here that wants money. I have come fourteen miles at the highest speed my horse would go. Said my husband, We are all ready to start to attend an important meeting, but were waiting for money. We shall not have time to catch the [train] cars now unless you take us. He did so, and we had just time to reach the cars, step upon the platform without purchasing tickets when the car started. This was the way the Lord educated us to trust in Him. In this way the truth has entered many places. Our faith and trust in God have been tested and tried again and again. For years we labored constantly to carry forward the work under the pressure of feebleness and great poverty.—**Manuscript 19, 1885 (Ellen G. White manuscript written in Basel, Switzerland, September 21, 1885).**

A patched coat and a three-foot trunk

While at Topsham [Maine] we received a letter from Brother E. L. H. Chamberlain, of Middletown, Conn., urging us to attend a conference in the State in April, 1848. We decided to go if we could obtain means. My husband settled with his employer, and found that there was ten dollars due him. With five of this I purchased articles of clothing that we very much needed, and then patched my husband's overcoat, even piecing the patches, making it difficult to tell the original cloth in the sleeves. We had five dollars left to take us to Dorchester, Mass.

Our trunk contained nearly everything we possessed on earth; but we enjoyed peace of mind and a clear conscience, and this we prized above earthly comforts. In Dorchester we called at the house of Brother Otis Nichols, and as we left, Sister Nichols handed my husband five dollars, which paid our fare to Middletown, Conn. We were strangers in Middletown, having never seen one of the brethren in Connecticut. Of our money there was but fifty cents left. My husband did not dare to use that to hire a carriage, so he threw our trunk upon a high pile of boards in a near-by lumber-yard, and we walked on in search of some one of like faith. We soon found Brother Chamberlain, who took us to his home. —White, *Life Sketches*, pp. 107, 108.

All we have including clothes, bedding, and household furniture we have with us in a three-foot trunk, and that is but half full. We have nothing else to do but to serve God and go where God opens the way for us.—**James White, letter to Brother and Sister Hastings, April, 1848, written from Middletown, Connecticut.**

Mowing for the Lord

It is rainy today so that I do not mow or I should not write. I mow five days for unbelievers and Sunday for believers and rest on the Seventh day, therefore I have but very little time to write. My health is good, God gives me strength to labor hard all day. I have mowed eight days right off and felt hardly a pain. Brother Holt, Brother John Belden and I have taken 100 acres of grass to mow, at 87 ° cents per acre and board ourselves. Praise the Lord. I hope to get a few dollars here to use in the cause of God.—**James White letter to "My Dear Brother" [Stockbridge Howland], July 2, 1848.**

In the summer of 1848, we received an invitation to hold a Conference with the few friends in Western New York. I was destitute of means, and with feeble health entered the hay-field to earn the sum necessary to bear our expenses to that meeting. I took a large job of mowing, and when fainting beneath the noonday sun, I would bow before God in my swath, call upon him for strength, rise refreshed, and mow on again. In five weeks I earned enough to bear our expenses to the conference. Bro. Bates joined us at this meeting. The notice had been given to all the Empire State who were in sympathy with our views, and there was general rally; yet there were not more than forty present.— **White, *Life Incidents*, p. 274.**

5

Commitment of Early Pioneers

John Andrews: Self-schooled for God's work

School was a delight to John. Early in life he made it a practice to rise at four o'clock in the morning and spend two or three hours before breakfast studying the Bible and praying.—**Virgil Robinson,** *Flame for the Lord*, **1975, p. 10.**

At the age of 11, having acquired a working knowledge of the three R's, John was forced to quit school because of poor health. From that time on whatever he learned he taught himself. Wherever he went he carried a book. Whenever there was a spare moment, no matter how brief, he would pull out his book and seek to absorb a few ideas from its pages.

Loving the Bible as he did, he naturally wished to read it in the languages in which it had been originally written. At his request his father got books in Greek, Latin, and Hebrew, which John studied diligently. One by one he mastered those languages. Before his death he was able to read the Bible in seven languages.—**ibid., p. 11.**

By the time he was 14 John was recognized as a powerful spiritual leader. He was often invited to address the people of Paris on the subject of religion. As he continued his deep study of the Bible he became more and more sure that Christ would return sometime in 1843 or 1844.—**ibid., p. 13.**

Annie and Uriah Smith: World without attraction

It will give our readers some idea of the sacrifices made by the workers in those early days to give a little of the experience of Brother [Uriah] Smith and his sister Annie in connecting with the Review Office. When they accepted the Sabbath truth, they had a standing offer to teach, in a new academy which was to be opened at Mt. Vernon, N. H., for three years at one thousand dollars a year, besides room and board. Seeing the need of such help as they could render in the office, they gave up the academy proposition, and came to Rochester, where they spent that three years in labor to advance the cause of present truth. For this labor they received their board and clothes. During this time all the laborers in the Review Office lived in the family of Brother [James] White, and all practiced the closest economy, thus saving all that could be saved to meet the expense of publishing the paper and tracts.

These workers were happy, and even esteemed it a privilege to sacrifice. The feelings of Brother and Sister Smith are well expressed in words penned by Sister Annie herself respecting her feelings at that time: "Earth has entirely lost its attractions. My hopes, joys, affections, are now all centered in things above and divine. I want no other place than to sit at the feet of Jesus, and learn of him, — no other occupation than to be in the service of my Heavenly Father,—no other delight than the peace of God which passeth all understanding." From association with Brother Smith in those early times, I know it was this same spirit of consecration that gladdened his heart.—**J. N. Loughborough, "Reminiscences of the Life of Uriah Smith,"** *Review and Herald*, **April 7, 1903, p. 8.**

Hiram Edson: A farm for a press

[A] big conference was held March 12 to 15, 1852, at Ballston, New York (or others have it as Ballston Spa, New York). At this time, [Hiram] Edson was still living on his farm at Port Byron [New York] which he had purchased. With all of his traveling, I don't see that he had much time to work it, though possibly he couldn't do much in the middle of winter anyway.

This was a very important meeting at Ballston. Among others, Brethren Bates, Rhodes, Holt, Wheeler, Day, Baker, Ingraham, Wyman, Churchill, Morse, and Edson were present. They came together "to be united in the TRUTH . . . not to establish any peculiar views of their own."

The conference was held in the home of Jesse Thompson. According to one account, James and Ellen White were also present at this meeting. Though these early pioneers were very poor (the Whites were using borrowed furniture in their home at the time; Bates had spent his fortune; young J. N. Andrews had neither scrip or purse; Rhodes and Bates, who were traveling far and wide, were both dependent upon the meager support of their hearers). Yet, on Friday, March 12, 1852, the subject of printing a paper came up for discussion. It was decided to purchase a press and type and to set this printing office up at Rochester where the *Review* would then be published.

It was a monumental decision for this small group to make. It was thought that $600.00 would be needed to purchase the press and type. A committee of three consisting of Brethren Pool, Drew, and Edson were to receive the money and to purchase the type and press. Edson's daughter, who was at that meeting with her parents where they were discussing the buying of the small Washington hand press, reports that her father said, "We, no doubt, will have a power press before the close; maybe two or three." It certainly must have required a lot of faith to have made a statement like that at that time. Of course he never expected time to go on this long, but wouldn't he be shocked to see our great presses of today printing our truth-filled literature for the people of the world!

The money was to actually be sent to Hiram Edson at Port Byron. It was at about this time that Edson sold his farm at Port Byron for $3500.00, and advanced $650.00, to purchase the press and type. To support himself and his family, he then rented a farm. He was to be paid back as donations came in from other believers for the press.—**James R. Nix,** *The Life and Work of Hiram Edson*, **unpublished term paper, 1971, pp. 59-61.**

6

Happenings in Rochester, New York

Labor without pay

[When James and Ellen White first moved to Rochester, New York, they lived at 124 Mt. Hope Avenue. Their rent was $175 per year. As the number of people living in the house increased, the printing press was eventually moved to South St. Paul's Street, Stone's Block, No. 21, Third Floor. The October 14, 1852 issue of <u>The Review and Herald</u> was the first to carry the new address.]

On May 6, 1852, the first number of Volume III of the *Advent Review and Sabbath Herald* was published in Rochester, N. Y., and was printed on a press and with type owned by Seventh-day Adventists. Hiram Edson had advanced means to purchase a Washington hand-press, with type and material for fitting up the office. He was to receive his pay as donations should come in from the friends of the truth. That hand-press now stands in the office of the *Review and Herald* at Battle Creek, Mich.,[36] and is regarded as the best proof-press in the office. In No. 12, Vol. III, Oct. 14, 1852, an announcement was made that the cost of fitting up the office with this press and material was $652.93, and the receipts for that purpose up to that date were $655.84. Of those twelve numbers of the paper, 2000 copies of each number had been issued and circulated gratuitously. In the business notes on the publisher's page of that number, we read:

"The office is not in debt, however, for this reason: Brethren [Stephen] Belden and [Oswald] Stowell, who have worked in the office the past six months, have received but a trifle more than their board. Others engaged in the same work, have received no more than they have. It will certainly be a pleasure for all the friends of present truth to help to make up the deficiency in the receipts, that those who have labored hard, especially in our absence, in the midst of sickness, in publishing the *Review and Herald*, may have comfortable support."—**Loughborough,** *Seventh-day Adventists*, **p. 167.**

Turnips for potatoes

Those who have labored in connection with the office, have been willing to sacrifice their time and ease. That the expenses of the REVIEW might not exceed its receipts, they have been willing to labor for a trifle more than their food and clothing, and this too, when their services elsewhere, or in other kinds of business, would command good wages. Some of them in coming to labor in this office, have, for that very purpose, left businesses that would command twice or thrice what they had offered them here. Beside this, they have been willing, not only to labor hard, but also to toil early and late, frequently till midnight, and on some occasions all night. And this they have cheerfully done that the truth might be published before the world. In addition to the above, that the expense of life in the city might be as small as consistent, those engaged in the office, with one exception have formed but one family. This has made the expense of publication less, but it has been attended with many inconveniences to all concerned. —**Affairs Connected with the [Publishing] Office,** *Review and Herald,* **December 20, 1854, p. 150.**

In April, 1852, we moved to Rochester, N.Y., under most

discouraging circumstances. At every step we were obliged to advance by faith. We were still crippled by poverty, and compelled to exercise the most rigid economy and self-denial. I will give a brief extract from a letter to Brother Howland's family, dated April 16, 1852:

"We are just getting settled in Rochester. We have rented an old house for one hundred and seventy-five dollars a year. We have the press in the house. Were it not for this, we should have to pay fifty dollars a year for office room. You would smile could you look in upon us and see our furniture. We have bought two old bedsteads for twenty-five cents each. My husband brought me home six old chairs, no two of them alike, for which he paid one dollar, and soon he presented me with four more old chairs without any seating, for which he paid sixty-two cents. The frames are strong, and I have been seating them with drilling. Butter is so high that we do not purchase it, neither can we afford potatoes. We use sauce in place of butter, and turnips for potatoes. Our first meals were taken on a fireboard placed upon two empty flour barrels. We are willing to endure privations if the work of God can be advanced. We believe the Lord's hand was in our coming to this place. There is a large field for labor, and but few laborers. Last Sabbath our meeting was excellent. The Lord refreshed us with His presence."—**White, *Life Sketches*, p. 142.**

Beans, beans, and more beans

Janie Fraser was young, buoyant, and energetic, but she was not what one would call a trained cook. Though she did not understand the desirable balance of proteins, fats, and carbohydrates necessary to be maintained, yet she fully understood the value of inexpensive foods, and especially of porridge and beans. She was a steadfast economist, and knew that a dollar's worth of beans would go farther in the feeding of a family of fifteen or more persons, seven of whom were hearty men and boys, than a dollar's worth of any other food.

After Uriah Smith had been in the family for a few weeks, he remarked to a comrade, that though he had no objection to eating beans 365 times in succession, yet when it came to making them a regular diet, he should protest!—**William C. White, "Sketches and Memories of James and Ellen G. White," No. XIV, Beginnings in Rochester, *Review and Herald*, June 13, 1935, p. 10.**

Binding with a shoemaker's awl

I often think of the time when Elder [J. N.] Loughborough, myself, and a few others, in Rochester, N.Y., under the direction of Brother [James] White, were preparing the first tracts to be sent out to the people. The instruments we had to use were a brad-awl, a straight edge, and a pen knife. Brother Loughborough, with the awl, would perforate the backs for stitching; the sisters would stitch them; and then I with the straight-edge and pen-knife, would trim the rough edges on the top, front, and bottom. We blistered our hands in the operation, and often the tracts in form were not half so true and square as the doctrines they taught.—**Uriah Smith, "History and Future Work of Seventh-day Adventists," *General Conference Daily Bulletin*, October 29, 1889, vol. 3, no. 9, p. 105.**

The laborers in the office of publication in those "pioneer days" had a very different prospect before them than the workers have at this time. No tithing system had as yet come to us. There was no fund from which salaries could be assured for services rendered. The facilities with which the work was to be performed, including hand-press, type, etc., had been purchased (new) for less than seven hundred dollars. Well do I remember when the first pamphlet was printed in the Rochester office, in the winter of 1853-4. It was a book of about eighty pages, on the sanctuary and twenty-three hundred days, written by Elder J. N. Andrews. The sheets were printed on the hand-press. A number of the believers in the Rochester company united with the office workers in folding, stitching, covering, and trimming these books. The office had no folding machine, no stabbing machine, no stitching machine, no paper cutter. The sisters folded and gathered the signatures, the writer stabbed the books with a shoemaker's pegging awl. After they were stitched with needle and thread, Sister Mary Patten (afterward Mead-Sawyer) pasted on the covers, and Brother Uriah Smith trimmed the edges with his pocket-knife, while Brother and Sister James White wrapped and directed advance copies to our people in other places. It was a happy day indeed, and why should it not have been? "The office of the Seventh-day Adventists was issuing its first pamphlet, printed on its own press."—**J. N. Loughborough, "Reminiscences of the Life of Uriah Smith,"** *Review and Herald,* **April 7, 1903, p. 8.**

The lock business God would not bless

For three and one-half years I had preached more or less among the First-day Adventists, but supporting myself principally by my own hand labor, as they had no direct system of ministerial support. I was convicted of duty to preach the third angel's message, but reasoned that it was so sacred a work that it might be better for me to labor for the support of myself and wife, and earn means with which to help others to preach the truth.

I had when I accepted the truth [in 1852] . . . about thirty-five dollars in hand. I still made earnest efforts to push the window-lock business in which I had previously been quite successful. As I went from place to place with the business, the conviction was constantly pressing upon me to make known to others the truths I had learned. With all the earnestness that I put forth, my business would not prosper. I could not succeed in making sales to builders who admitted that the locks which I was handling they would finally put into their buildings. In some instances my sales for a week (five days) in such places as Lockport, Medina, and Middleport,[37] would only give enough profit to pay my hotel bill and fare to and from Rochester [New York].

This state of things soon consumed what money I had saved, leaving me in a situation where I had not money enough to pay the fare out of Rochester. All this time, which covered the rest of

October, November, and the first of December, 1852, the conviction fastened itself upon me more and more deeply that I must give myself wholly to the preaching of this truth. Finally, about the middle of December, my money was reduced to a silver three-cent piece[38]. As I attended the next Sabbath meeting, a cloud seemed to hang over the meeting. As prayer was offered for the removal of the cloud, Sister White was taken off in vision. Then she had a message for me. On relating the vision she said: "The reason this cloud hung over the meeting, is that Brother Loughborough is resisting the conviction of duty. God wants him to give himself wholly to the preaching of the message." I did not then take my stand to do it, for I could not see how I could be supported in so doing. On reaching my home, it was with a heavy load resting upon me. I said to myself, "This thing has got to be settled." I retired to my chamber and there told the Lord if He would open the way I would go out; but that did not settle it. Finally, on the strength of the Testimony, I said, "I will obey, Lord, and Thou wilt open the way." At once all these harrowing and perplexing doubts passed from my mind, and I was happy in the thought that the Lord would provide, notwithstanding I had but three cents, and knew not where another cent would come from. I arose from my knees with the full assurance that the Lord would open the way as I should move in the direction of duty.

On the Monday morning following, my wife,[39] who did not know how low my funds were reduced, came to ask me for money with which to get matches and some thread. I said, taking the money from my pocket, "Mary, there is a three-cent piece. It is all the money I have in the world. Only get one cent's worth of matches. Spend only one of the other cents, and bring me one cent, so that we shall not be entirely out of money." Said I, "Mary, I have tried hard, every way in my power, to make this business succeed, but I can not." With tears she said, "John, what in the world are we going to do?" I replied, "I have been powerfully convicted for weeks that the reason my business does not succeed is because the Lord's hand is against it for neglect of duty. It is my duty to give myself wholly to the preaching of the truth." "But," she said, "if you go to preaching, how are we to be supported?" "Well," said I, "as soon as I decided to obey the call of duty, there came to me the assurance that the Lord is going to open the way; I don't know how it will be done, but the way will open." She retired to her room to weep, and perhaps to pray. At least I saw no more of her for an hour. Then she went out to make her little purchases. In our next article we shall see how this came out, and how the tide turned.—**John N. Loughborough, "Sketches of the Past.-No. 74,"** *Pacific Union Recorder*, **July 29, 1909, p. 1.**

In our last article we left our narrative with my wife out making her purchases of matches and thread, spending two cents of my last three cents. At the same time I was studying the message, happy in the Lord with the assurance that He would open my way to speak the truth. I of course pitied the poor wife's humble necessity of making, with so sad a heart, such small purchases. Not more than thirty minutes from the time she left the door suddenly there was a loud rap. On going to the door there stood a gentleman, who inquired, "Does Mr. Loughborough live here?" I assured him that I was the man, and invited him to come in.

Seating himself, he said, "I am Mr. _____, from Middleport.[40] I am not in very good health, and am going to the state of Ohio for my health. I wished to take along some small business with which to meet expenses. I was recommended to you by Mr. Thomas Garbutt (Mr. G_____ was a First-day Adventist minister) to purchase some of Mr. Arnold's patent sash-locks. I am going out to Penfield,[41] some seven miles[42] in the country, and will be back to-morrow noon. I want eighty dollars' worth of locks, and will leave you to pick out an assortment, as you have retailed the locks. I will take the locks to-morrow and pay you the money." All I would have to do would be to walk half a mile[43] to the factory and leave the order. They would bring the locks, with a little model window with which to illustrate their use, to my door. My commission on such a sale was one third of the gross receipts. So here would come into my hands twenty-six dollars. This sum would go as far in making purchases for the family and table in that time as three times that amount would purchase now.

Very soon after the man left, my sad wife returned with her purchases and my one cent, but she found me . . . singing. She said, "You seem to be very happy," "O yes," I said, "I have had some company since you left, and the Lord has opened the way for me to go out and preach the third angel's message." With this I told her what had happened, and in a flood of different tears, again she retired to her room to weep and seek the Lord. She came back soon, as happy as I, and ready to do what she could to prepare me for my labors. On receiving my money, I very soon purchased wood, provisions, and what was necessary for home comforts as I should enter the field.—**Loughborough, "Sketches of the Past-No. 75,"** *Pacific Union Recorder*, **August 12, 1909, p. 1.**

[What follows is an account of J. N. Loughborough's ministerial "training"]

The above-related experience brought us to the third Sabbath in December (1852), the next Sabbath after I decided to give myself to preaching the message. On that Sabbath there was a general gathering at 124 Mt. Hope Avenue, of the Sabbath-keepers of western New York. In the opening prayer of that meeting Sister White was again taken off in vision. Among other things presented to her, she said to me, "You are correct in your decision to give yourself to the work of the ministry. It is now your duty to go on, and tarry no longer." In that meeting prayer was offered for me that the Lord would further open the way before me to go.

Brother Hiram Edson, who lived some forty miles[44] east of Rochester, had decided not to attend that meeting; but his wife had been so impressed that he was going be called away that she had all his clothing in shape for any emergency. On the said Sabbath morning, while engaged in family worship, the impression came upon him as strong as though spoken with an audible voice, "Go to Rochester, you are wanted there." He said to his wife,[45] "What does that mean? I do not know why I should go to Rochester." All the day the impression came stronger and stronger. Several times in the day he retired to his barn to pray, and every time the impression would come, "Go to Rochester."

Finally he said to Sister Edson, "Is my clothing in a condition to leave? It is my impression that I am to be gone several weeks." She assured him that all was ready, for she had been impressed that he would be called somewhere. After the close of the Sabbath he took the cars[46] for Rochester. On arriving at Mt. Hope Avenue about nine o'clock at night, he said to Brother White, "I did not expect to come to this meeting, but I have been impressed so strongly to-day that I should come here that here I am. What do you want of me?" "Well," said Brother [James] White, "we want you to take old Charlie horse and the carriage and take Brother Loughborough around on your six-weeks' circuit in southwestern New York and Pennsylvania, and get him started in preaching the third angel's message."—**Loughborough, "Sketches of the Past-No. 75,"** *Pacific Union Recorder*, August 12, 1909, p. 1.

7

The Battle Creek Years

[Late in 1855, James White moved the press from Rochester, New York, to Battle Creek, Michigan, where the name "Seventh-day Adventist" was chosen in 1860, and the General Conference was organized in 1863.]

The gift of four

There were four men in Michigan, of whom Henry Lyon was one, who built the financial platform for the transfer of the denominational headquarters to that State. When Joseph Bates met them in Jackson in 1852, he remarked that all of them except "the first named" [Henry Lyon] were "professed public teachers, and feel the burden of the third angel's message." Henry Lyon may not have been a public teacher; though if his daughter Angie was a sample, the gift ran in the family (perhaps through his wife); but he was evidently a man of vision and of executive ability. When James White visited Michigan in 1853, and gave the modest suggestion at Battle Creek that if the brethren were faithful, they might create quite a company to represent the cause in that village, he had not yet reckoned with Henry Lyon.

It was a year later when Lyon came to Battle Creek, five years before its incorporation as a city. He kept his eye on the work of God, and judiciously gave of his means to it. His mind was busy with plans for its extension; and in consultation with his energetic son-in-law[47] he conceived the idea of bringing its headquarters west. As his town grew in every direction, Henry Lyon, working at his trade, saw its extension northwest in his own section, and he said, "Why not Battle Creek?"

By the time the Whites visited Michigan again, in April of 1855, the plan was perfected. Lyon had consulted with Dan R. Palmer, the blacksmith of Jackson, and with Cyrenius Smith and J. P. Kellogg. The last named had been his country neighbor, who sold his farm soon after Lyon did, and moved to Jackson, where he engaged in the making of brooms. Smith likewise sold his place, and moved to Battle Creek about the time of the transfer, and Kellogg came later; but Palmer stayed in Jackson. However, the four made up a fund of $1,200, even shares from each; and with this the brethren in Michigan proposed to James White to purchase land and erect a building in Battle Creek for the printing plant and publishing office of the *Review and Herald.*

It was an offer which appealed to James White. He had begun the publishing work with no capital but faith; he had carried it from place to place where his pilgrim stems had gone; he had borne it on his heart while traveling and preaching and writing, often bowed down under sickness and misfortune. He had more than once declared to his brethren that he could no longer carry it, and they had responded, according to their lights and their ability, by helping him. But there was no organization; that had been beyond their ken and against the prejudice of many of them. White had owned no property; the publishing business had begun in an attic[48] and continued in his rented homes, with hired printers, until the purchase of a press and its location in Rochester [New York], but still only in leased quarters. Now the Michigan brethren proposed not only to build a home for the paper, but to stand behind it with their counsel and cooperation and money. Not yet did they see the way clear to incorporation of the business; that was to come later. But their sturdy shoulders were put to the wheels; and James White, with his brethren and co-workers, accepted gladly.

This twelve-hundred-dollar gift is a landmark in Seventh-day Adventist history. Small as it may now appear, it was great in proportion to the resources of the people then; and, if we except [Hiram] Edson's advancement of funds for the first press [in 1852], it was the primary constructive effort in the building of a world-wide work.—**Arthur W. Spalding, *Origin and History of Seventh-day Adventists*, vol. 1, 1961, pp. 266-268.**

During the year following their acceptance of Adventism, the [John P.] Kelloggs sold their farm and moved to Jackson. Here they enjoyed the fellowship of a larger group sharing their religious convictions. John Preston, returning to an old family trade, began to make brooms to support his family. The Kelloggs devoted a substantial portion of the $3,500 they had received from the sale of the farm to promoting their new faith. With three other Michigan Adventists, John advanced $1,200 to move the Review and Herald publishing plant from Rochester, New York, to the little Michigan community of Battle Creek. He also made a sub-stantial contribution toward the purchase of the first tent secured by Adventists for public evangelism in Michigan.—**Richard W. Schwarz, *John Harvey Kellogg, M. D.*, 1970, p. 13.**

Buck and Bright are pullin' away

The spirit of the givers is reflected in the case of a farmer near Battle Creek, Richard Godsmark, whose work stock, as with many of his neighbors, consisted of a yoke of oxen. He had no money to give, but, eager to have a part, he sold the pair and gave the proceeds for the press. And every time he stumped to town in his cowhide boots he made sure to go by the printing office, and, stopping to listen to the roar and clack of the power press, he would exclaim gleefully, "Buck and Bright are pullin' away; they're pu-u-ullin' away!"—**Spalding, *Seventh-day Adventists*, vol. 1, p. 277.**

Baptisms in icy holes

In one of the school districts in M[onterey, Michigan] we commenced a series of meetings on the evening of the 14th,[49] and continued until the evening of First-day,[50] 18th, notwithstanding the extreme cold weather at the time, the most of the church in M. attended every evening, traveling from six to ten miles[51] out and home. Their prayers, and spirited exhortations, and singing, both before and after preaching, stirred up the people in the district, and some deep and hearty confessions were made, and strong desires to hear and examine more fully this important subject, while some others fully decided to keep the Commandments of God, and the Faith of Jesus.

On First-day morning, (mercury 30 degrees below zero,[52]) some of the Brn. in the time of service cut and sawed out the ice some three feet thick, and found water of sufficient depth, wherein seven souls were buried with Christ in baptism.[53]—**Joseph Bates, "Letter from Bro. Bates,"** *The Review and Herald*, **Feb. 19, 1857, p. 125.**

A name above reproach

All accounts and traditions concerning Elder Bates agree as to his benevolent attitude toward both men and women. Unlike some of his more jovial fellow workers, he never joked, but his genial speech and manners made him a most agreeable companion. In the matter of propriety he stood so erect that some felt he leaned over backward. One time he visited the Stites family out in the country near Battle Creek, Michigan. Mr. Stites was ill. There were no sons in that family, but two daughters in their teens, the older of whom was Mary, my wife's mother, who told us the tale. When Elder Bates was to leave, the younger girl, Deborah, harnessed the horse to the buggy, to take him to town. Courteously he thanked her, but said, "My daughter, the Bible tells us to avoid the very appearance of evil. There are wagging tongues in the world, and a young woman must keep her name above reproach. Just now it is in my keeping, and I can not allow you to drive me in." So, despite their protests, he picked up his heavy satchel and footed it to town. —Spalding, *Seventh-day Adventists*, appendix note for page 40, vol. 1, pp. 395, 396

Section III

ADVENTISM GOES WEST
1868

1

Sabbath Keepers Settle in California

A Snake and a Sabbath nap

When I engaged to take the frieght through to Pikes Peak[54] I drew up a contract in which it was expressly stated that the team and wagon were to be at all times under my control and that we would not travel on Saturday, as that was the Sabbath day. All parties agreed to this and Capt. Parks signed the contract, he being the chief man of the party of five.

The first Friday night after leaving Columbus,[55] we camped at a fine place in which to spend the Sabbath, expecting to remain there until Sunday morning. All parties were agreed to do so, until a wagon came up and camped near us. A man by the name of Esther owned the outfit. He had with him his wife and child and a Mr. Ide, his wife's brother, and a young man. This party were all old acquaintances of Capt. Parks, and as they were going to Pikes Peak, Capt. Parks asked me next morning to hitch up and travel with them. This I could not conscientiously do, and I so told the captain. Upon finding that I would not go on, he began to talk with my wife to get her to insist that I go on. He represented to her that it would be dangerous for us to travel alone, as we were liable to be attacked by Indians at any time. (We had not seen an Indian since leaving Elk Horn.[56]) He finally got her so frightened that she wanted to go on, but I would not consent. I told him that I would travel as far Sunday as they could Saturday, so that we could camp together every night except Saturday. This did not suit him, however, and, asking the four other men to help him, he hitched up and drove on, although I forbad it and told them to remember how our contract read.

When I found they would go on I took my Bible and a lunch, and my pistol, and stayed behind. After they had passed on, I walked down to the Platte River one mile[57] distant and waded across a narrow and shallow branch, onto a wooded island and spent the day there. The sun shone quite hot at midday, and I began to feel drowsy. So I closed my Bible and using it for a pillow, soon fell asleep. I did not sleep long, however, for I was suddenly awakened by a hissing noise, and, opening my eyes, I beheld a snake's head within three inches[58] of my face. The head was fully three inches wide and five inches[59] long and was the most frightful sight I had ever beheld. With a sudden bound, I sprang fully five feet[60] and grabbed a club with which I speedily put the snake out of commission. This snake was of an unknown kind, to me at least, and was the largest I had ever seen except at a show. It was six feet[61] long and three inches thick.

I did not go asleep again that day, nor did I see any more snakes.

About two hours before sunset, I discovered a large wolf about a quarter of a mile[62] away. . . . An hour later, two more wolves put in their appearance at the spot where I saw the first one. . . . A few minutes later I started for the road, which I reached just as the sun was sinking below the western horizon.

I had seen a string of four wagons pass along the road at about noon, so I expected to reach their camp about eight or ten miles[63] ahead. As soon as I reached the road I took a dog trot, which I did not break until I reached my own company, at half past 10 P. M.[64]

On reaching camp I found all was well excepting that one of the men had lost my ax in the river, while attempting to wade to an island to get wood to cook supper with. This was a great loss to me, as I could not procure another and had only a small hatchet with my tools.

The men did not attempt to interfere with the team again, nor did they again ask me to travel on the Sabbath. Sometimes the wagons would all stop over both Saturday and Sunday. Whenever they went on the Sabbath, we would lay by and then catch up with them while they lay by on Sunday.—**Merritt G. Kellogg, M. D.,** *Notes Concerning the Kelloggs,* **1927, pp. 69-72.**

In March, 1859, M[erritt] G. Kellogg, half-brother of Dr. J. H. Kellogg, started from Michigan with his family and a chest of carpenter tools, by team, expecting to secure work in some of the Western States. At Platte River, Nebraska, he fell in with a company forming to go to California. Substituting oxen for horses, he joined the company of emigrants. As he was a good mechanic, he felt confident that in those stirring times of emigration to the "Golden State" he would experience no difficulty in securing labor for the support of his family. After a trip of about five months, fraught with some difficulties because of his determination to carry out the agreement made by the company that there should be no traveling on the Sabbath, they arrived at Marysville in the autumn of that year. He broke from the company, remaining in the vicinity of Marysville till the fall of 1860, when he passed on to San Francisco, immediately receiving employment at good wages.

Not long after his arrival in San Francisco, Brother Kellogg formed acquaintance with B. G. St. John, who came from New York City in the early days of the gold excitement. In 1843-44 he was an earnest Adventist in New York. He still believed in the near coming of Christ, but had not as yet had opportunity to hear the third angel's message. Brother Kellogg found this family ready listeners to the sanctuary question, the third angel's message, and the Sabbath truth. They introduced Brother Kellogg to some of their Baptist friends, who also began the observance of the Sabbath. About 1864 Brother J. W. Cronkrite, a shoemaker, came from Michigan, *via* the isthmus, to San Francisco, thinking to support himself by his trade, and by the circulation of tracts do some missionary work. These few souls had Sabbath meetings in the home of Brother St. John on Minna St. In their anxiety to see the message proclaimed to the public, this company raised $133 in gold, and forwarded the same to Battle Creek, accompanied with an earnest request for a minister to come. The money was receipted in the *Review* of December 11, 1866. In the same paper Elder [James] White said to the donors, "Do not be discouraged; we believe in due time the Lord will provide men and means for the proclamation of His truth in California."

When the question of health reform was agitated in our papers, Brother M. G. Kellogg became deeply interested in the study of the same, and cherished the thought of going East to study medical science. Having succeeded in accumulating, by carpenter work, several hundred dollars, he went, in the year 1867, *via* the isthmus, to take a course of study for the winter at Dr. Trall's College, Florence Heights, N. J. Before entering upon his studies, he visited Battle Creek, Michigan, for the purpose of making a personal plea for the work in California. Of this visit, in the *Review* of November 12, 1867, Brother White said: "We have had a visit the past week from M. G. Kellogg, who has been for the last nine years in California, keeping the Sabbath, and thus by his example, and publications from the office, letting the light of the message shine. Quite a number, as a result, are keeping the Sabbath. He designs to return in the spring; and should he do so, we trust he will be able to take some help to that promising field." —**Loughborough**, "Sketches of the Past-No. 139," *Pacific Union Recorder*, June 19, 1913, pp. 2, 3.

They went two by two

[The decision to send missionaries to officially open the work in California was made at the 1868 General Conference Session in Battle Creek, Michigan.]

During the winter of 1867-68, the writer, having made Battle Creek, Mich., his home for ten years, was much exercised in mind with reference to changing his field of labor. Much prayer ascended heavenward over the subject, and impressions became more and more forcible that the place of labor would be at the southwest, and a long distance at that. Still seeking for wisdom and guidance, the Lord gave the writer as many as a score of dreams, in which laboring in California with a tent and otherwise figured largely. . . .

As it afterward developed, the mind of Elder D. T. Bourdeau was exercised in a similar manner, and so certain was it settled with him that he was to be sent to some distant western field and not return to Vermont that he sold his all, horse, carriage, and household goods, coming to Battle Creek with his wife to attend the General Conference, having all his worldly effects in bank drafts, and holding himself ready to go where the General Conference and the providence of God should indicate.

When the conference convened in May, 1868, Brother M. G. Kellogg was present, and presented a strong plea for a laborer to be sent to California. In those times, when our field of operations was limited, and about every minister attended the General Conference, the mode of procedure to the distribution of laborers was to call for a report and applications for labor from the different fields. Then the president of the conference would ask all the laborers to seek the Lord earnestly for guidance, that the mind of each might be clear as to the field he should occupy. In a day or two the ministers would be called upon to state the particular field to which the Lord seemed to be leading them. This course was pursued in that conference. When the report was called for on May 18, one after another arose and stated his conviction. This went on till every special call had been supplied, and all the ministers reported except Elder Bourdeau and the writer. No minister had as yet said anything about the California field. Elder [James] White then said, "Has no one had any impressions of duty with reference to the California field?"

Then, for the first time, the writer arose and stated his impressions and dreams with reference to the California field. With this the sense of the body seemed to be that the Lord's time had come to open up the work in California. Brother White then remarked, "When the Lord sent forth His servants, He sent them two and two, and it seems as though two ministers should go to that distant field. Is there no other one whose mind has been led to that field?" Then Elder Bourdeau arose and stated how his mind had been exercised, and that he had come to the meetings with his companion and all his earthly substance ready to go where the conference might say. Thus the meeting for distribution of labor closed. Brother White said, "Will Brethren Bourdeau and Loughborough pray over this together and separately until the day the *Review* goes to press, that they may be sure of the mind of the Lord in the matter?" We most earnestly sought the Lord, and as we would meet the word of each was, "California or nothing." On the morning of May 31, the day the *Review* was to be printed, Brother White said, "Brethren, what is the decision?" Our united reply was, "California or nothing." He at once penned the statement for the paper, calling for $1,000 to secure a tent, and to send Elders Bourdeau and Loughborough to California. He said his mind had been settled in the matter for several days. He had only waited for our decision.—**Loughborough, "Sketches of the Past-No. 140,"** *Pacific Union Recorder*, **July 3, 1913, p. 5.**

A cross-country travel bargain

When, in the spring of 1868, the decision was made to open up the work on the Pacific Coast, the overland railroad was not completed, there being an unfinished gap of five hundred miles[65] between the Union Pacific and Central Pacific roads. Our only course was to come by steamer from New York to Aspinwall,[66] cross the isthmus by rail to Panama,[67] thence by steamer to San Francisco. While we were waiting for our tent to be made in Rochester, New York, and otherwise preparing for our journey,[68] there was a peculiar providence which greatly favored us in point of means.

A Mr. Peters, of Battle Creek, who had been three times across the isthmus, said to the writer: "You will do well to go to New York and secure your tickets several days before you expect to sail. You will find on the Pacific Mail line the best accommodations. There is another line, the American, which runs a boat between the sailings of the mail line, and there is considerable competition for transportation between the days of the mail line sailings. You go to New York the day after the mail line ship has sailed. Go to the office of the American line and get their best figures for their next saling. Then with these figures go to the mail line office, and they will give you good terms, much lower. As for your freight, instead of taking it with you, ship it to New York by Wells Fargo, to go as slow freight to California. It will get there about two weeks after your arrival, at a cost of about one third what it would be to go with you."

We followed Mr. Peter's advice. We learned that tickets bought on the day of the steamer's sailing, cabin fare, were $160 for adults, and one fourth that amount for children three and one half years old. This would have been a total for our company of $680. On going to the American line, the agent said he would carry the adults for $129 each, and the boy for $32.00, which would be $548 for all. With these figures I went to the office of the Pacific Mail line. Their steamer for the next trip, the "Rising Star," lay at the wharf by the side of the office. I was the second one who had applied for passage. The agent took me aboard the ship and let me select good rooms near the center of the ship, and offered to take us all for $467.50. This was $212.50 less than we would have paid had we not been advised by Mr. Peters, for we were planning to go to the steamer and secure our tickets on the morning of the sailing. All this was saved by a trip from Victor [New York] to New York [City] and return, at a cost of $17.00.

Wednesday, June 24, our steamer left New York City, and we arrived and landed at Aspinwall on Friday, July 3, at 9 A. M. At eleven o'clock we were on our way to Panama [City] by rail, where we arrived at 4 P.M., and were immediately taken by tugboat to the steamer, which was anchored about one mile[69] from the shore. We were told that the steamer would soon be off for California. Instead of that, our boat lay at anchor until Sunday morning, July 5, at 4 A. M.

The cause of the delay was this: This steamer, the "Golden City," was the largest the company owned. The next steamer to make the trip was a small one; so the company took on all the slow freight it could well store to make it easier for the next ship, and to relieve waiting freight.

Our passage from New York to San Francisco, over 6,000 miles,[70] was quite pleasant, especially on the Pacific. Our steamer came to the wharf in San Francisco at 10 A. M., Sabbath, July 18, being twenty-four days from New York. As Brother [M. G.] Kellogg had given us the address of Brother [B. G.] St. John's family, on Minna Street, with the assurance that they would entertain us until we could make further arrangements, Brother Bourdeau went at once to prospect, while I remained with the family until the trunks came from the steamer. He soon returned, stating that he found the few Sabbath-keepers (consisting of Brother St. John, his wife and two daughters, Brother [J. W.] Cronkrite, and a Brother Moon,—two who were to leave for the States on Monday's steamer) assembled for a meeting, which they had adjourned until we should arrive. An expressman took us and our trunks to Brother St. John's, where we were made welcome, and we at once had a brief Sabbath meeting as our first introduction to California.—**Loughborough, "Sketches of the Past-No. 141,"** *Pacific Union Recorder*, **October 30, 1913, p. 1.**

A dream of two men

An incident occurred in connection with the opening up of the work on the Pacific Coast which well illustrates how the providence of God may be working and preparing the way before His servants while they are pleading for His guidance, and when, as yet, they know nothing of it.

When Elder James White made the call in the *Review* for $1,000 to send Elders Bourdeau and Loughborough to California with a new tent, one of the New York City journals immediately grasped it as a news item, and inserted it as such in their paper, stating that two evangelists were about to sail to California to hold religious services in a large tent. The papers containing this item reached California several weeks before our arrival.

There was at that time in Petaluma a company of worshipers who called themselves Independents. This company was composed of those who had separated themselves from the various churches, feeling that they could not fellowship the formality and pride found in them. They appeared to be a very earnest, devoted people, who worshiped in a hall which they had erected. When they saw the notice of the evangelists coming to the state with a tent, they said:

"It may be the Lord is sending these men with their tent to do a work that needs to be done on this coast." They at once began to make the matter a subject of prayer. The tenor of their petitions was this: "If these, O Lord, are Thy servants, give them a prosperous journey, and come Thou with them."

There was one of their number, a Brother Wolf, who was very earnest, and to whom the Lord had seemed to give at different times very impressive dreams, which had proved of so much practical utility that the company had much confidence in them. After one of their special praying seasons, this Brother Wolf had a very striking dream. He saw in his dream gloom and darkness settled all over the surrounding country. While considering this, he saw two men kindling a fire, which made a brilliant light, and brought cheer to the inhabitants. As this fire blazed brightly, his people were rejoicing for the light that had come into their midst. At this point he saw all the ministers in Petaluma come with brush, straw, and tufts of grass, throwing them upon the fire, trying to extinguish the flames. The more they tried to put out the fire, the brighter it burned.

While these ministers were busy trying to put out this one fire, the men had started a second. The minister endeavored in the same manner to extinguish the second fire, but with no better success than had attended the first effort. This process was repeated until the two men had kindled five fires, and much light was shed in the hitherto darkness. The ministers had tried in vain to quench the flames of all five of the fires. Then he saw these ministers in counsel over the matter and overheard them saying: "There is no use of our trying publicly to oppose these men, for they get the advantage of us every time. We will let them alone, and cease to oppose them publicly." From that time they left the men with their fires alone.

Then the brother was informed in his dream that these two men were the two evangelists who were coming with the tent, and as a company they must help them. He was bidden to take a good look at the men, so that he would know them when he should see them. He related his dream to that company, who believed it was from the Lord, and decided to help the men when they should come, and, if possible, get them to begin their tent work in Petaluma.

Just after the brother related his dream, the town of Petaluma was placed under quarantine for smallpox, so that no meetings of any kind were held for several weeks. Brother Wolf told his people that he must see these evangelists on their arrival, for if they were the men he saw in his dream, he would surely know them. Of all this we knew nothing until some time after opening our meetings in Petaluma.—**Loughborough, "Sketches of the Past-No. 142,"** *Pacific Union Recorder*, **November 27, 1913, pp. 1, 2.**

We were not expecting our tent until two weeks after our arrival in San Francisco. What was our surprise, on the morning of July 20, as Brother Bourdeau and I took a walk to the Pacific Mail wharf, on entering their warehouse, to see that the sacks containing our tent had come on the same steamer with us! Here was another providence. Our tent was among the extra freight put on at Panama to lighten the load of the next steamer coming to San Francisco, so we paid only slow freight rates for what had really come as fast freight.

As our tent had arrived, we hastened to get our side poles, ropes, lamps, and fixtures ready for commencing tent meetings somewhere. We had the tent conveyed to Brother St. John's house, and began to study and pray over the matter as to where we should erect it. The few Sabbath-keepers in the city were anxious that our first effort should be made there. When we prayed over the subject, our minds were impressed to go to the northwest, and away from San Francisco. Brother St. John would say, "The direction in which you point must be Sonoma County, but we want the tent erected here."

We then began searching for a suitable lot on which to erect the tent in the city. With all our searching, we found but one place that could be secured. That belonged to a Jew, who said he wanted to sell the lot, and would not let us have the use of it for less than $40 a month. That settled the question about beginning a tent effort in San Francisco at that time. I had held tent meetings for fourteen years, and never had paid a dollar for the use of the ground on which the tent stood. Our decision was then made to go out of the city with our tent. But the question was, Where?

Thus matters stood until July 27, when Brother Hough, one of the independents from Petaluma, Sonoma County, called at Brother St. John's, and inquired if there were two ministers stopping with him who had come from the States with a tent. When he met us, he said he belonged to a company of worshipers in Petaluma who had learned that two ministers were coming to the state with a tent, and that company had delegated him to come to the city and invite us to pitch our tent first in Petaluma.

How did he so quickly find us in a city numbering at that time 175,000 inhabitants? On his way down to the city, it was impressed on his mind to go at once to the Pacific Mail wharf, and inquire if a tent had come on their last steamer from Panama. Being informed in the affirmative, he inquired, "Where was the tent taken?" As he asked that question, the very drayman who had moved the tent came into the warehouse. He said that he moved the tent to such a number on Minna Street. So in about thirty minutes from the time Brother Hough landed in San Francisco from the Petaluma steamer, he had found us.

We went to Petaluma the next day. On our arrival, Brother

Hough met us and said: "You will stop at my house to-night, but it is arranged for you to take dinner at Brother Wolf's. I will go with you there, and come for you after dinner." We learned afterward that this was arranged so that Brother Wolf could see the two men, and know for a certainty whether they were the ones he had seen in his dream. He said to his wife, as he saw us coming with Brother Hough: "Wife, *there they are*. Those are the *identical* men I saw in the dream." That settled the matter with that company, and they did what they could in securing for us rooms in which to live, and in arranging for the tent meetings. On the 29th of July, we returned to San Francisco, and prepared to move our effects to Petaluma, which removal was effected on August 3. We settled for housekeeping in furnished rooms belonging to Sister Otis, one of the company of independents, and prepared as rapidly as possible for opening our meetings at Petaluma, a town that had for a month been quarantined for smallpox, our tent effort being among the first public gatherings after the quarantine was lifted. **—Loughborough, "Sketches of the Past-No. 143," *Pacific Union Recorder*, February 12, 1914, pp. 5, 6.**

The Independents in Petaluma furnished ground, stakes, etc., for our tent; but we still needed lumber for seating, so Brother Hough introduced me to Mr. Rice, the lumber dealer in town. I told him that in the States we usually had the use of lumber from the yards free, simply paying for what was cut or otherwise damaged on return of the same.

"Well," said he, "I don't know about trusting a minister with lumber. My experience with them has taught me that they are rather a risky set of men. At least we have found it so here in California." With a smile, I said, "Mr. Rice, you may not find them all alike." After looking me over squarely, and seeing I took no offense at his remark, he replied, "I will let you have a thousand feet of lumber if Mr. Hough will go security for it." That seemed a little rough on us, but I thanked him all the same for the accommodation.

Our service in the tent opened Thursday evening, August 13, with a crowd of attentive listeners. On our arrival at San Francisco, we had received a testimony from Sister White. It was instruction given to her in vision at Battle Creek, while we were in the state of New York waiting for the completion of our tent. It related to the manner of labor in California. Letters at that time came across the five hundred miles of uncompleted railroad by "pony express," while all heavy mail came by sea. So the letter was awaiting our arrival.

Brother Bourdeau and I had both labored in the New England States, where great economy was exercised to make, as they expressed it, "both ends meet." The testimony to us said: "You can not labor in California as you did in New England. Such strict economy would be considered 'penny wise' by the Californians. Things are managed there on a more liberal scale. You will have to meet them in the same liberal spirit, but not in a spendthrift manner." It was our study how to apply this instruction.

We had brought a few pamphlets and tracts with us with which to begin our work, leaving a heavier shipment to come as "slow freight," because all baggage over the one hundred pounds allowed to each adult passenger was charged ten cents a pound for crossing the isthmus by rail to Panama. The smallest coin used in California at that time was ten cents. When persons saw our tracts at one and two cents apiece, they inquired: "Do you expect to sell these? There are no cents in circulation here." Our reply was, "We can give them away then."

On the first Sunday morning, we placed our books and tracts hundred pages to a package. That Sunday the minister of the largest church in the place had asthma, and so dismissed his congregation without services. Many of his members came to the tent. One among them, a Brother Moore, said, "If they tell us when the world is coming to an end, I will get up and tell them they do not know anything about it." As the members from the church came in, they took their position on the front seats. The congregation listened to the singing of pieces, all new to them, in which we carried all four parts. With deep interest they listened to the singing, and gave earnest attention to the word spoken.

Just before closing the service, I remarked that we had some reading-matter on the subjects we were presenting. "Here," I stated, "is a set of pamphlets, comprising five hundred pages, for fifty cents a package. Brother Bourdeau will give the tracts at his end of the stand to all who will receive them." Brother Moore arose, took a package of the books, and laid down two half-dollars on the stand. I said, "We will sell them after the close of the service." He replied, "I was afraid I would not get any." After the service, I said to the brother, "The books are only fifty cents." He replied, "A dollar is cheap enough." As Brother Bourdeau was handing out his tracts, one man said: "You can't afford to give away tracts for nothing. Here's a dollar. Give away a dollar's worth for me." Another handed him fifty cents, others quarter-dollars. In less time than it takes to write this, our stand was cleared of books and tracts, and the congregation was going from the tent with expressions of favor for the new ministers that had come among them.

So opened our first tent meeting in California. After the close of the tract distribution, Elder Bourdeau found that the people had handed him more money than the retail price of the tracts given away.—**Loughborough, "Sketches of the Past-No. 144,"** *Pacific Union Recorder*, **March 19, 1914, pp. 2, 3.**

2

Pacific Press, Oakland, California

Aggressive leadership of a chosen man

The first issues of the *Signs of the Times* were sent to a list of prospective subscribers compiled by Elder [James] White's son J. E. White, including all Western subscribers to the *Review and Herald*. The paper was offered for $2 per year to those who chose to pay. Others could receive it free as far as the generosity of "friends of the cause" would permit. Thus the missionary status of the journal was established at the start, and the circulation was determined largely by the amount which church members were willing to give. An appeal was made for addresses in the hope that copies of the paper could become available to all who were interested. Funds were called for to pay for this free distribution.

Now comes a demonstration of the aggressive leadership of James White. In a note in the first issue, which he signed as president of the Seventh-day Adventist Publishing Association, he suggested that for $2,000 he could buy all the materials necessary to print the *Signs* and that, after starting publication, he would turn all equipment over to a publishing association if one could be formed on the Pacific Coast. He recalls that he did this when the Publishing Association was formed in Battle Creek in 1861 for the publication of the *Review*. Readers from coast to coast were urged to sustain the *Review and Herald* and at the same time to help the new paper.

One week later James White's hopes had risen. In the second issue he asked for 10,000 subscribers to the *Signs* money or no money, and he wanted 100 donors of $100 each to buy a steam press and accessories. Eight $100 donors were already listed, including James White, Ellen White, and J. N. Loughborough. The growing list was published in each succeeding issue. In the fifth issue the $10,000 for a steam press had grown to $20,000 to build and equip a printing plant. One thousand dollars had already been paid for materials to use in setting up forms ready for hired press-work.

The third annual session of the California State Conference convened on October 2, 1874, at Yountville, during the camp meeting. On the third day Elder G. I. Butler, a General Conference delegate, read a message from Elder James White, who was in Battle Creek and had been elected for a second time as president of the General Conference. The General Conference, it said, had voted a donation of $6,000 to buy a steam press and other equipment for printing the *Signs of the Times*. Elder White had planned to take personal charge of the Western publication, but since new duties would call for his continued presence in the East, it was suggested that the California Conference take charge of the publication. The gift and the responsibility were accepted. The Conference committee agreed to purchase the *Signs* and assume control "until such time as a legally organized Association shall be formed and its officers elected."

Now came the problem of raising the funds for a building. The conference president, Elder Loughborough, went to the people at the camp meeting, asking for at least $10,000. The conference had already voted to raise $1,000 for an evangelistic tent. That need was also presented at this meeting. The result in pledges as $19,414 for the *Signs* and $1,616.20 for the tent. There were two gifts of $1,000 and several of $500, but the rest was in smaller amounts. Here was a typical example of large-scale Western thinking and giving. Then it was voted to donate $500 from the state funds to the General Conference. This gift was gratefully received, but it was returned to the California Conference the next February in view of the needs of the West.

Such generous giving was in addition to the regular systematic benevolence funds, amounting to more than $4,000 per quarter, missionary subscriptions to the *Signs*, and other freewill offerings. It will be recalled that the membership in California was less than 500. The General Conference session of August, 1875, listed California membership at 450, and Western membership between Mexico and British Columbia at 1,000. No wonder a news reporter, noting the figure $19,414, asked Elder M. E. Cornell if the amount given for publishing was $1,900!—**Richard B. Lewis, *Streams of Light, The Story of the Pacific Press*, 1958, pp. 3, 4.**

Humble people moved by faith

"Among the stories my [Alma McKibbin's] parents told me in my early childhood was one of a camp meeting held at Yountville . . . . The matter of special importance at this meeting was the need of a paper in which the publish the Biblical truths which were so precious to them and which they felt it was their duty to share with the world.

"My parents had but recently come from the Middle West, where money of any kind was scarce, especially gold coin. When the people were asked to contribute to this contemplated enterprise, my father, looking about over the assembled congregation, said to himself: 'These people will not give enough to buy the ink for the first edition.' But the hands that went into the pockets of blue jeans or the folds of print dresses brought out not silver, but gold—gold coins and, more amazing still, unminted gold in bars and wedges. Soon thousands of dollars lay heaped upon the rostrum—the gifts of a humble people moved by a great faith."

In a few minutes the gold and pledges amounted to $19,414. When the date came that the pledges were due, January 1, 1876, the sum of $20,000 had been paid into that fund. That same day at the camp meeting $1,616 was also pledged for a campmeeting fund. Referring to this generosity, [Eld. G. I.] Butler wrote:

"We have financial strength in this state sufficient to do almost anything we wish to undertake. There is a stability to this cause here; it is of no mushroom growth. When responsible persons come forward and pledge over $21,000 of yellow gold to sustain and forward the work going on in its midst, all will agree that it means business. It is no wonder that ministers and members of our staid, respectable popular churches are astonished at such a result."—**Harold O. McCumber,** *Pioneering the Message in the Golden West*, **1968 ed., pp. 102, 103.**

[A] camp meeting was held at Yountville. That's about sixteen miles[71] from St. Helena. So my family[72] packed up. I was Grandma's special charge. And because of my thin skin[73] . . . she made a little bonnet for me and she held an umbrella over me all the way there. And yet, when I arrived there my cheeks were burned. She went some distance away to a farmer, got some cream and put it all over my face, and she made a little mask for me, because she wanted to go to the meetings. [She] took a piece of muslin and cut eye holes in it, and fastened it around my head. She'd sit way in the back of the tent, while father and mother sat up in front. It was at that meeting that they gave their $14,000 to establish a printing establishment on this coast. Well, I was there. If you'd been there you would look way in the corner, you would've seen a little baby girl with a mask over her face, being cared for by a dirty old grandma. . . .

When I look at that picture, [You know, they have a picture[74] of people going up and giving their contributions], Grandma said that when some of them laid down a little piece of metal, . . . she whispered in my ear "Gold." I'd been in . . . California [long enough] to know gold. You know, they had no printing presses[75] here, so they just went and made it into wedges. [When] someone put down a gold wedge, I applauded. . . . —**Alma McKibbin, excerpt from oral history interview done with James R. Nix, August 2, 1967.**

Keep shoveling that coal

In the summer of 1876 I joined the *Signs* as a volunteer. At that time the mailing list had grown too large for the carpet bag, and we (W. C. White and the writer) carried the weekly mail to the post office in a large market basket and a bundle which was easily carried under my arm. . . .

The next job for us two boys was to keep steam up in the little upright donkey engine. When the [press] run called for one or two hundred extra copies, and the boys in the pressroom geared up the old drum cylinder press, we boys put an extra weight on the safety valve and shoveled more coal. . . .

Often do I recall the pioneer editors and writers. They wrote by hand; no fountain pens or stenographers. I can still see some of the "copy." Once, in the summer of 1879 or 1880, I went to the editor's room and knocked on the door. No response. I opened the door, and there on his back on the floor lay the editor, sound asleep. Evidently he had been up all night writing. I tiptoed around him to his table (no desk), picked up the copy, and took it down to the composing room, where I was told that the article was to be in the next week's *Signs*. Those men were hard workers, and full of zeal. . . .—**Reminiscences of W. E. Whalin quoted in McCumber, *Golden West*, 1968 ed., pp. 104, 105.**

Section IV

PERSONAL COMMITMENTS
1863-1915

1

John N. Andrews

A Bible scholar

His study of the Bible was so thorough, and his knowledge of its contents so complete, that, he told me in confidence, were the New Testament to be destroyed, he thought he could reproduce it word for word. He also informed me that he read the Bible in seven languages with a clear understanding.—**John O. Corliss, "The Message and Its Friends-No. 5, Andrews, Its Pioneer Missionary," *Review and Herald*, September 6, 1923, p. 6.**

Not satisfied with reading the Bible in English only, he read it with clear understanding in French, German, Greek, Latin, and Hebrew.—**Robinson, *Flame for the Lord*, p. 101.**

A man of prayer

When Elder J. N. Andrews was writing on his "History of the Sabbath" in Battle Creek, for economy's sake he occupied a bed in the recess of the editorial room of the Review office. During the working hours this room was so public that there was no privacy for prayer. Elder Andrews said he must find a place where he could pray for divine help when his mind was not clear as to just the best way to express his thoughts.

He searched through the building, but could find no place for retirement except in an attic, where back numbers of the periodicals were stored. This he converted into his sanctum, and frequently we would see him winding his way through the composing room to an almost perpendicular ladder which led to that dimly lighted, ill-ventilated place, where he would spend hours pleading for wisdom to present correctly the truths that have since enlightened the world regarding the history of the Sabbath.

This made a profound impression on my young mind. O that his example might be followed more closely by us all!—**M. S. Boyd, "The First Italian Tract,"** *Review and Herald*, **September 18, 1924, p. 61.**

First official overseas missionary

A camp-meeting was appointed to convene a short distance west of Battle Creek, in the summer of 1874, just prior to the departure of our first missionary to a foreign field, and Elder Andrews was present. When the expansion of the message was dwelt upon, and notice was given that he would soon leave for Europe, a change came over the meeting, and Elder Andrews, who had never before appeared so solemn, at once seemed altered in appearance. His face shone with such pronounced brightness that, as I saw him and heard his apparently inspired words of quiet contentment to be anywhere with the Lord, I thought of the story of Stephen and his wonderful experience when before the Jewish Sanhedrin. God was evidently preparing him for an ordeal that none of us had ever known or suspected.

I had never before witnessed a sight so heavenly, nor have I seen anything equaling it since that time. I have, however, thought that before the Master returns to earth for His own, some will behold glory in a larger and brighter form even than that which enshrouded Brother Andrews on that memorable occasion. May that time hasten!—**Corliss, "The Message and Its Friends-No. 5,** *Review and Herald,* **September 6, 1923, p. 7.**

Although only eleven years old when Elder J. N. Andrews went to Europe, I remember it well. At this time it is difficult for people to understand how the believers were stirred by this event. It was talked over and over for a long time. The next summer, at the Wisconsin camp-meeting, Elder James White told the familiar story of carrying the first copy of the *Present Truth* to the post office in a carpetbag, and then, with a voice tense with emotion, he exclaimed, "Now we have a missionary over in Europe." It was a soul-inspiring story.—**Mrs. L. B. Priddy, "A Bit of Church History,"** *Review and Herald,* **September 18, 1924, p. 59**.

The paper [*Les Signes*] was costing more than Andrews had expected. If there was one thing he hated more than another, it was to have to ask for money. He would rather go without necessary food and clothing than to write to the General Conference asking for funds. When he went to Europe the brethren didn't set any specific salary for him. They wanted to find out how living costs there would compare with those in the United States.

So, instead of setting a salary, they agreed to send him money from time to time. Unfortunately, during the first two or three years those times were few and far between. To publish tracts and pamphlets, and later on *Les Signes*, Andrews had to go into debt for three or four months at a time. Little by little he withdrew his own money from the bank and used it to meet living expenses. Sometimes he was several months behind with his rent.

Faced with the expenses of a trip to Italy to see Dr. Ribton, Andrews wrote a letter to Elder James White, "If you think proper to do so—send me $500 or $1,000." Ellen White read this letter, and beneath the signature she wrote and underlined, "Please send immediately."

James White knew that Elder Andrews would need more and more money, so he made another appeal in the *Review* for the expanding work in Europe. This brought in $2,000. And the General Conference committee voted to raise $10,000, but it was many months before this money arrived in Europe.

On January 13, 1877, John Andrews was struck down with pneumonia. He would shake with cold chills, then he would perspire with burning fever. After this had continued for a week, a doctor was called. He gave the minister a thorough examination.

After he had finished, the physician pointed to the minister's gaunt face and exclaimed, "This man is almost starved to death!" It was all too true. In order to have money to use for the work, Andrews had often gone without necessary food. His temperature continued to rise, and he lost consciousness. For many days he was very sick. Then gradually he began to recover.—**Robinson, *Flame for the Lord*, pp. 101-103.**

In 1877 Brother and Sister William Ings and I arrived in Switzerland to assist Elder Andrews in establishing our printing work in Europe. One small room — a bedroom — in the mission home was dedicated to the setting of the type and making up of the forms. When they were in readiness, they were taken in a handcart to the city by Brother Charles M. Andrews, where the printing was done.

Our facilities were meager indeed, as far as mechanical apparatus was concerned. They consisted of a few fonts of type, sufficient to set *Les Signes des Temps* and a few tracts in French and German.—**Boyd, *Review and Herald*, September 18, 1924, p. 61.**

Cleansed through the blood of Christ

On July 22 [1883] he wrote in his diary, "Today I enter my fifty-fifth year. My life seems wholly filled with faults. I pray that I may be thoroughly cleansed in the blood of Christ."

Realizing that the time would soon come when Elder Andrews could no longer direct the work in Europe, the General Conference appointed Elder B. L. Whitney to go to Basel and prepare to take over. Someone suggested that John's aged mother, Sarah Andrews, go with Elder Whitney to be with her son. Before deciding, George I. Butler, president of the General Conference, wrote to Elder Andrews and asked his permission. At first John said he didn't wish his mother to come.

"I would rather not have her see me in my present feeble condition," he wrote. "It would only bring sorrow to her heart. If I must die, let it be alone."

Elder Butler wrote and explained to Elder Andrews that his mother would like nothing more than to be able to minister to her son. When Ellen White was asked about the move, she wrote to Elder Butler, "Sister Andrews should be with her son." Reluctantly John gave his consent.

When Elder Whitney sailed for Europe, Mother Andrews, Mrs. Martha Andrews, the widow of John's brother, William, and Martha's daughter, Sarah, were with him.—**Robinson, *Flame for the Lord*, p. 120.**

In May, 1881, J. N. Loughborough, our senior Seventh-day Adventist minister, then in charge of our mission in Great Britain, came to Basel to see his old colleague and friend. The particular object of this visit was to have a period of consultation and special prayer that the Lord would graciously restore the health of Brother Andrews. This visit (which reminds me of Farel's visit to Calvin in his sick room at Geneva) must have been a great source of comfort to the lonely publisher.

The following year, missionaries laboring in Switzerland, Great Britain, and Scandinavia felt the necessity of coming together for mutual instruction and encouragement. They therefore met at Basel in September, 1882, under the chairmanship of Brother Andrews, A.A. John acting as secretary. S. N. Haskell, having just terminated a visit to these different European missions, was present. He was another former colaborer [sic.] of Elder Andrews, and his visit was greatly appreciated.

Seeing the need of larger quarters for the work and the

increasing family of workers, Elder Haskell rented a new building twice the size of the former place, and as the sick missionary in his condition would have shrunk from the idea of moving, he had the tactfulness to have the moving done while the two friends were taking a pleasant little trip together.

Before his departure, Elder Haskell attend the annual meeting at Tramelan. Though hardly able to sit up, Elder Andrews presided. I shall never forget the prayer that Brother Haskell offered in his behalf on that occasion in the public schoolroom. It was a mighty supplication, a humble and at times a despairing cry to God for help and relief, a clinging to the throne of the Infinite. The congregation, though unacquainted with English, were sobbing. Heaven seemed near to bless.

Another profitable visit in the spring of 1883 was that of Dr. J. H. Kellogg, back from a trip to Vienna for special study, and whose affable and generous manners were long remembered by all the mission household. He was so struck by the intensity of Elder Andrews' interest in his work and of the largeness of his plans and hopes, that he wrote to America that everything possible must be done in order to save the missionary's life.

This pathetic appeal had its effect. On July 26 of the same year, a venerable-looking American woman, eighty-three years of age, slowly made her way to Elder Andrews' sick room. The writer was in the building, but did not witness the meeting of Brother Andrews and his aged mother. She was accompanied by Elder Andrews' sister-in-law, Martha Butler Andrews, and her little daughter, and also with a special friend of his, B. L. Whitney, his wife, and two daughters. Nothing more could be desired by the solitary and exhausted pioneer, as far as human friendship and tender affection were concerned. He seemed to revive, and probably spent his reserve strength in instilling into the hearts of his newly arrived friends his own enthusiasm and hopes. Many prayers ascended to God for his recovery. Every earthly means was used to that effect. But the reaction soon appeared. His strength gradually gave way, and his faithful pen itself refused to obey.

From one week to another the publication of the paper was delayed, in the hope that he might be able to write his articles for the August number, the second issue of the eighth year. This was no mean task, as shown by the list of his articles in the preceding number. They were as follows:

1. The Return of Israel.

2. Communion With God.

3. The Book of Zechariah (Ch. 10).

4. Will the Second Advent Be Silent and Invisible? (First article.)

5. Conditionalism in the Holy Scriptures.

6. The Six Days of Creation. (First article.)

7. The First Day of the Week in the Early Centuries. (A historical series.)

These articles make a total of twenty-two to twenty-three solid columns.

Thus, physically exhausted, but with a mind "as clear as a bell" (to use his own expression), he was able to write five Biblical studies, one historical study, and an article on practical Christianity. But he had to submit to God's will. In a short notice he welcomed the "arrival of Pastor Whitney," his successor, and added another short notice, saying:

"This number of *Les Signes* had been delayed by reason of the grave illness of the editor, who has been suffering seriously with lung disease for the last four years. It seems now certain that he will soon be obliged to leave the entire management of *Les Signes des Temps* to other hands."

Facing the stern reality, the sick man now entered into a period of mental struggle of which some faint idea was gathered by his friends. Then came a period of excruciating physical pain, in which he was heroically supported by proclaiming aloud the sublimity and perfect sufficiency of the Christian religion.

But relief came, and with it perfect submission, perfect peace.

All anxiety about his work, all sorrow over his unfinished task, disappeared. He told his friends that he felt as if carried down a deep and surging stream, while his feet rested on the rock beneath. "The storms have abated," he said, "I am nearing land. God is good, God is infinitely good, infinitely good, infinitely good."—**Jean Vuilleumier, "Early Days of the Message in Europe-No. 4,"** *Review and Herald***, April 18, 1929, p. 10.**

Into this editorial work went all there was of Elder Andrews' declining strength. For each issue, he usually wrote four or five strong Biblical articles, dealing with various phases of present truth and Christian living. The last number he wrote was the one for July, 1883. In this issue are found no less than seven important articles from his pen, besides eight short notes.

Until the middle of March, 1883, Elder Andrews was able to be about. On Sunday night, February 25, he attended a large meeting held in a popular hall, in which Elder Erzenberger reviewed a sermon preached against the Sabbath of the fourth commandment by a leading minister of Basel. A great victory was scored for the truth. Elder Andrews sat on the platform with the speaker, to give him his moral support at a critical time; but his weary, careworn, emaciated features indicated that he was a wounded soldier and that it meant heroism for him to be on the battlefield.

And now I will quote from my diary:

"APRIL 15, 1883.—The paper was mailed three days ago. Elder Andrews is very weak since he wrote his articles. They were written in a short time, and with relentless perseverance. He seems exhausted from the effort, having lost his appetite in consequence.

"APRIL 25.—Elder Andrews is very weak. The manner in which he has been able to do his work the past few months is simply miraculous. He was saying to us the other day, 'You see me now in my natural condition. I have no strength left. If God did not raise me up from month to month as you would raise a man lying on his back, I could not do anything. When I have written my articles, I am left prostrated as you see me.

Then I cry to God, who sends His angel to strengthen me until my articles are written. But I do not know whether He will do this any longer. Dr. Kellogg (who was then traveling in Europe) tells me that, from the human standpoint, I have nothing but death to expect. As far as I am personally concerned, the future never seemed darker.'

"MAY 6.—During the past week, Elder Andrews has written only a page, and that with great difficulty. Each day, though extremely weak, he has asked for his paper and ink, and has tried to write. At night he had written only a few lines. But he does not want to give up. Every morning he dresses, and comes into the dining-room, his German Bible under his arm. His tall, slender form drops on a chair. But he scarcely eats anything. 'If I could only eat,' he says, 'I think I could write, but it won't go down.' Then he will lean his forehead on the table, and sometimes tears will flow down his hollow cheeks.

"Last night I went in to see him. He was lying down. His eyes were moist. He began to speak about his work, and added, 'If God does not give me strength to write for this number, I shall take it as a sign that I must die. The reason why I would be sorry to die now is that I have in those boxes a large quantity of important manuscripts which I would like to finish . . . . If I die, all this will be lost, for those who shall come after me will not know of their existence. But it may be better for me to lie down, and I must pray God continually to help me to be resigned to His holy will.'

MAY 11.—Last Tuesday, at dinner time, Elder Andrews seemed to have reached the limit of physical weakness. He could eat nothing. Several times he stretched out his hands, closed his eyes, and repeated the words, 'My God, have mercy upon us.' Then he said, 'It may be that it is God's will that I should die. His will be done! God is infinitely good.'

"In the afternoon he tried to write, but in vain. Finally he undressed and went to bed. At four o'clock the sun shone brightly into his room. He got up and dressed again, and then he remained a long while breathless in his armchair. As his son (Charles M. Andrews) then entered his room, he asked him for the board on which he writes on his lap, and for paper and ink. An hour later, as I heard him coughing and praying, I went in. 'Well,' he said, 'I have written two pages. What do you think of that?' and then he told me the above.

"MAY 23.—Elder Andrews has finished writing all his editorials, seven long articles, and a short one on socialism. As the paper was almost all set up without his contributions, and we were short of type, Edward (Borle) had to distribute some Italian tracts and work early and late to make time. The number printed was 5,500, one extra thousand being paid for by Dr. Kellogg.

"JUNE 20.—Our June number is nearly finished. In great weakness, Elder Andrews has written several articles. He has even begun a new series in answer to an attack on immortality through Christ by Mr. Luigi in the *Eglise libre*.

"JUNE 28.—Our June number is printed and mailed. It should have been sent out on the first.

"JULY 13.—Elder Andrews told me yesterday that unless a miracle takes place in his behalf, he must soon die. He has insisted on vacating his room in view of the soon arrival of his aged mother from America. Today he has written his article on the 'Return of the Jews.' Pastor Byse, of Brussels, writes that he is pleased with Elder Andrews' reply to the *Eglise libre*. Pastor Edward White, of London, has also written, saying that he wished that our paper were published in English. He knows of no paper that equals it.

"JULY 16.—We have sent out the third and last free copy to our 5,000 list, and we are now preparing a new list including forty-seven villages.

"JULY 18.—Elder Andrews has written his editorial on sanctification and his series on Zechariah. He intends now to write on refuting the invisible coming of the Saviour. The paper should have been ready one month ago. It is only half made up. Sabbath, Elder Andrews told me that if he could not write on Sunday, he would give up the effort, and have the paper completed with extracts. He has received word that a party consisting of Elder Whitney, president of the New York Conference, and his family, his own mother, his sister-in-law, Martha Andrews (*nee* Butler), and her daughter Sarah, are in England on their way here. He is very anxious to see them arrive.

"JULY 25.—Elder Andrews has written a little, but he has been most of the day on his back, having eaten nothing. At 4 P.M. he sent me to buy him a certain kind of buns, saying, 'Perhaps, after I have eaten them, I can finish my article on the so-called "Invisible Translation of the Church."' At night the article was all written. And now he has an intense desire to write a second reply to M. Luigi's attack. He feels a great responsibility to complete the promised refutation, which is being watched for by some prominent men, such as Pastors White and Byse.

"Today the answer was all ready in his mind, but 'nature gave up.' 'When this is done,' he said, 'I want to write an article on the history of Sunday in the Christian church, one on the doctrine of the Sabbath, and some other things. But through how much suffering, even if I succeed!'. . .

"'I have written to the brethren in American that I have upon me a heavy burden which I can neither carry nor lay down.' He smiled sadly, and he added, 'As I think of it, sometimes I shed tears.' He began to weep; but soon recovering himself, he said in French: 'Malgré cela, je ne suis pas triste ni mélancolique; non, je remets toutes choses entre les mains de Dieu.' (For all this. I am not sad nor melancholy. No, I rest everything in God's hands.)

"SABBATH, JULY 28.—The long-expected missionary party from America arrived Thursday in the evening. I have had the great pleasure of meeting them all: Elder B. L. Whitney, Mrs. Whitney, their two daughters, Jean and Lenna, grandmother Andrews (aged 83), Mrs. Martha Andrews, and her little daughter Sarah. Brother Andrews got up the next morning and spent the whole day in conversation with Elder Whitney.

"AUGUST 9.—Brother Andrews finds himself unable to write (for the August number).

"AUGUST 12.—Elder Whitney is absent, visiting the churches. Elder Andrews, unable to write, has had a long conversation with Sister Whitney.

"AUGUST 14.—Today I told Elder Andrews that a subscriber had written that he liked the article on Israel very much, and that he was praying God for the recovery of our dear editor. He exclaimed: 'Good! That's good!'

"AUGUST 22.—Our dear brother has been lying helpless on his bed for the last sixteen days. He has not been able to write anything for this month's issue. It being very late, it had to be set up in a hurry after it was evident that Elder Andrews could not contribute anything. It is made up of good extracts and quotations, but the living issues, which are the life of the paper, are absent. Will those important series remain unfinished?

"(NOTE.—Brother Andrews last effort to write is probably a blank sheet of paper in my possession on which he wrote the title of his third article on 'Conditionalism in the Scriptures.')

"SEPTEMBER 5.—Elder Andrews keeps failing. He speaks about his funeral. He has a great desire to labor on, but if God has otherwise decided, he wished to die at an early date, 'if I can be ready.'

"SEPTEMBER 7.—A marked change is noticeable in Elder Andrews. His present state of mind shows the power of the grace of God. He feels the blessing of God in a special manner. He has laid all his burdens on the Lord. All the cares and anxieties of the mission, which were resting on him, he has intrusted to Elder Whitney's hands. He is calm and quiet. He feels the burden no more. Today, when Sister Andrews and myself were in his room, he touchingly said: 'I have reached a point which I compare with a vessel nearing port. It is no longer in mid-ocean, open to the fury of the storms. The cliffs of the shore keep off the winds, the sea has become quiet, the waves vanish, the calm appears.' His voice, scarcely audible, made his words all the more impressive. Then, addressing his sister-in-law, he added: 'Martha, my life has been a total failure. There is not one among those who have endeavored to spread the truth who has failed as I have. Nearly all my efforts for the advancement of the truth have come short, and what I have done has not borne the fruit that I expected. May God forgive me!' To which Sister Andrews replied: 'But you have the consolation of knowing that what you have written is being circulated to the world, and that the people are being enlightened by it.' 'Oh,' he said, 'what I have written will soon be forgotten.'

"OCTOBER 7.—The last few days a severe diarrhea has threatened to terminate the life of Elder Andrews. But prayer was offered in his behalf, and God intervened graciously. He was telling us tonight that he is feeling the Lord very near. 'God is holding my hand,' he said. 'Although going down the stream, my feet have not lost the bottom. They are still resting firmly upon the Rock of Ages.' The other day he said to us, 'It seems to me that I cannot stop repeating, The Lord is good, the Lord is good; oh, what goodness, what goodness, what goodness!'

"OCTOBER 25.—On Wednesday, October 10, in the evening, we learned that Elder Andrews was growing worse. He suffered severe pain. His prostration was complete. Elder Whitney spent the night with him. The next day at noon I saw his mother and his son both weeping in the hall. Drawing near the door of his room, I heard groans. His mother invited Edward [Borle] and me to step in. Elder Andrews was lying on his bed uttering deep groans. He held his hand out to us, and said in French: 'Be ever faithful to God, my young brethren; that is the essential thing.' The groans increased; the sick man wrung his hands and rolled on his bed. We all dropped on our knees and prayed, he following us with a few words of prayer, expressing the fullest submission and resignation to God.

"Elder Whitney, having entered the room, was standing by the bedside with his hand on Elder Andrews' forehead. 'The pain intensifies, intensifies,' moaned the sick man, and he added, his hands outstretched: 'O God! Have mercy upon me in this my extremity!' Presently, he broke out, his voice rising gradually until it became a long, loud, triumphant shout: 'I am satisfied, *satisfied*, SATISFIED with the Christian religion!'

Then he recited the scripture: ' "Yea, though I walk through the valley of the shadow of death; I will fear no evil: for Thou art with me; Thy rod and Thy staff, they comfort me." '

"My work called me away from the scene. During the afternoon, the pains subsided gradually. In the evening, Elder Andrews had some sleep. During the following nights, we took turns watching with him. Each time I had to assist him in any way, he said, 'I am sorry to give you so much trouble.'

"On the 18th of October, the brethren began to come in from a distance for the Swiss and general missionary conference which was to convene. Friday evening, the 19th, at the opening session, . . . the meeting hall was crowded. The Sabbath (the 20th) was a solemn day. In the morning, Elders D. T. Bourdeau and B. L. Whitney spoke, and a social meeting followed, which closed with a season of prayer for Brother Andrews.

"Sunday morning (Oct. 21), Elder Whitney summoned the leading brethren together at half past seven. After consulting, they went up to Elder Andrews' room (he had been transferred to a larger room a few days before the conference), where a season of prayer took place. Brethren Albert Vuilleumier, L. Aufranc, and James Erzenberger offered humble confession and earnest prayer in behalf of the dying brother. Brother D. T. Bourdeau followed, breaking down as he prayed. Brother Biglia (from Naples) prayed in French, and Brother Aslan, from Rumania, in Rumanian. Edward Borle and Elder Whitney closed the season of intercession. During this time the congregation downstairs were praying for the same object. At two o'clock there was a session of the conference."

Here, my diary ends, as far as Elder Andrews is concerned. He died at sunset of this same day, the 21st of October, 1883. About 4 P.M., a few brethren had again gathered around his bed, engaging in earnest prayer that, if it were God's will, our beloved brother might be restored to health and active service in His cause.

His venerable mother and his son were present. During all this time, Elder Andrews remained almost motionless, seemingly lost to his surroundings, sometimes whispering a few words in his mother's ear.

When we got up from prayer, the sun was setting in the cloudless west, its golden rays filling the room, while the aged lady was quietly fanning the face of her dying son. It was a scene of solemn stillness. Heaven seemed near. Presently Albert Vuilleumier, who was standing at the foot of the bed, took out his eyeglass, and looking intently at the tranquil face, exclaimed, 'Why, he is dead!' So he was. He had passed away so peacefully that not one among the bystanders had noticed it. It was the 21st of October, the very day on which he said, that morning, that he wished to die. [Elder Andrews probably thought it was the 22nd, as that was the day of the disappointment in 1844.—ED.]

As Elder Whitney wrote in his obituary notice: "He yielded his life, without a doubt or shadow, into the hands of the eternal Wisdom, and went to sleep as quietly as a child in the arms of his mother, the eyes fixed with perfect assurance on the glorious morning of the resurrection."

He was fifty-four years of age.

The golden evening brightens in the west,

Soon, soon, to faithful warriors comes their rest!—**Jean Vuilleumier, "The Last Days of Elder J. N. Andrews,"** *Review and Herald*, **September 18, 1924, pp. 56-59.**

When we arrived here, the 26th of last July, we found Bro. Andrews very feeble, wasted almost to a skeleton, able to take a few steps with great effort, and to sit up a little while during the day; yet at work whenever he had a little strength. He was finishing his articles for the July number of *Les Signes,* which was already much behind. The prospect of death seemed very near to him, yet he clung to the work, and to life for the work's sake. We persuaded him to omit his articles for the August issue, hoping he might gain a little strength, but he continued to fail, and if, at times, there seemed to be a brief truce with the dread disease, it was soon broken by the re-appearance of the severe symptoms, which left him each time weaker.

His pen, once laid down, was not taken up again, but he continued to read the proof of the paper, as had been his custom, lying in bed, in spite of the entreaties of all, that he would spare his strength. . . .

For some weeks he had been unusually cheerful and calm, willing to live or die, as God saw fit, and this feeling of cheerful trust seemed to deepen. Even in the midst of severe suffering he praised God and dwelt upon his mercy and love. The cares and burdens of the past were all laid aside, and though his interest in the work did not abate till he lost all consciousness of this world, he seemed to feel no anxious care. No murmur of impatience or complaint escaped him, even in the midst of severest suffering, but he expressed much affectionate gratitude to those who administered to his wants.

The Swiss Conference, which was appointed to meet here, assembled according to appointment, and I was necessarily much occupied, but found time to go to his room occasionally and assist in caring for him. He begged me not to leave the meetings to do for him, as his interest, he said was wholly in the meeting. Lying on his bed, away from the sounds of the meeting, he seemed to feel a constant sympathy with the work going on, and realized more than ever the blessing of the Spirit of God. Friday evening he said to his mother that he felt sure the brethren had been praying for him, for he felt such a blessing, and relief from suffering; and this was true. At the close of the Sabbath a special season of prayer was held for him in the meeting hall by the brethren and sisters assembled. In speaking that evening of his desires, he said that he would not, if he could, take the responsibility of deciding whether he should live or die. He would gladly live to work in the cause if that were God's will, but he was willing to die if God saw best. He felt that his case was wholly in the hands of the Lord.

Sunday morning, at his request, a few met in his room for

prayer, after which he seemed much relieved, although he continued to fail steadily through the day. Half an hour before his death he seemed to lose consciousness, and at five o'clock P. M.[77], he fell asleep without a struggle or a groan, surrounded by those nearest of kin, and those who loved him tenderly.

During the last two weeks of his life he had completed what business arrangement he had to make, and as his last act, about three hours before his death, with his own trembling hand, and with great apparent satisfaction, he assigned to the mission $500 of his estate not already disposed of.

His mind seemed clear as long as consciousness remained. It was a privilege highly appreciated by his aged mother to be able to minister to her only remaining son, in his last hours,—a service which was rewarded by his grateful affectionate appreciation. —B. L. Whitney, "Death of Eld. J. N. Andrews," *The Review and Herald*, November 20, 1883, p. 730.

In accordance with his written desire, no eulogy appeared in the *Review and Herald* that announced his death.— **Robinson,** *Flame for the Lord*, p. 122.

2

Mary Andrews[78]

Mary [Andrews] was not well. Little by little she was losing strength. No longer could she work for long hours in the publishing house. She developed a persistent cough and found breathing difficult. Elder Andrews took her to a local doctor. He pronounced the dread word, consumption, or tuberculosis as it is generally called today. John asked whether there was hope for her recovery. The doctor shook his head; there was no sure cure.

In September, Andrews received an invitation to attend the coming General Conference session to be held in Battle Creek. He decided to go and take Mary to the Battle Creek Sanitarium. Surely his good friend Dr. Kellogg would find some way to save a life so valuable to the work of God. Charles would remain with Elder Ings and keep the presses rolling.

He wrote to the General Conference of his plans, carefully pointing out that he would be responsible for the entire cost of getting Mary to Battle Creek.

Elder Bourdeau had decided to return to America, and would travel with him by the least expensive passage. There was so much work to be done before Andrews could leave Basel that he feared he might be late for the conference. By working night and day he managed to leave enough prepared material for two complete issues of *Les Signes*. Then he and Mary said good-by to Charles and boarded the ship for America.

The General Conference session opened on October 4. Elder Andrews arrived in Battle Creek the same day. In the afternoon he spoke to the assembled delegates and the Battle Creek church members. As he pointed out various countries in Europe that now had Sabbathkeepers, the people were thrilled. They marveled that he and his fellow workers had accomplished so much in just four years.

Elder Andrews lost no time in taking Mary to the Sanitarium, where Dr. Kellogg gave her a careful examination. The doctor was shocked to see how far the disease had progressed. Kindly and sadly he told John that, from a human standpoint, there was no hope for her recovery. She could not live for more than a month or two.

From that day on, the devoted father scarcely left Mary's bedside. Day and night he watched over her, doing for her everything that could make her comfortable. Dr. Kellogg warned Elder Andrews of the danger he was running that he might contract the disease himself. Nothing could persuade the father to leave the bedside of his loving, gifted daughter.

On the night of November 27, Mary Andrews died at the age of 17. She was buried in the Oak Hill Cemetery in Battle Creek.[79] A few days after the funeral Elder Andrews received a comforting message from Ellen G. White:

"In my last vision, I saw you. Your head was inclined toward the earth, and you were following in tears your beloved Mary to her last dwelling place in this world. Then I saw the Lord looking upon you full of love and compassion. I saw the coming of Him who is to give life to our mortal bodies, and your wife and children came forth from their graves clad in immortal splendor."

Elder Andrews found the loss simply overwhelming. For weeks he was prostrated with grief. So many of his plans for the work in Europe had centered in Mary. She had done the editorial work in the office, leaving him free to visit Sabbathkeepers in various parts of Europe.

Somehow he couldn't understand why he had been called to make such a sacrifice. To a long-time friend he wrote in his grief, "I seem to be having hold upon God with a numb hand."— **Robinson, *Flame for the Lord*, pp. 110-112,**

[Autograph album sentiment written by J. N. Andrews the day after Mary's death]

Yesterday morning at 4.30 my dear daughter Mary F. Andrews fell asleep in death. This child rendered me great assistance in Europe, and when we encountered privation and want she met all with invincible courage and with faith and hope. What she suffered caused her to fall by the quick consumption. She has fallen in the work at a time when her services had become of great value. Who is there that will rise up to take her place?

Battle Creek, Nov. 28   1878
J. N. Andrews

—The autograph album in which this is found is housed in the Heritage Room of the Loma Linda University Library, Loma Linda, California.

3

John O. Corliss

Shortly after [his] marriage, Brother Corliss started afoot for the northern part of Michigan, to engage in evangelistic work. No conference funds were then available, and he was not himself blessed with worldly goods. His worthy wife, however, engaged to cook for a crew of sawmill hands at two dollars a week, and so partially provided the necessary funds to keep him at his chosen calling. In addition to the funds supplied by his good wife's labors, he did work enough to keep his expenses fairly well balanced.—**J. L. McElhany, "Life Sketch of Elder J. O. Corliss,"** *Review and Herald*, **October 25, 1923, p. 19.**

4

Stephen N. Haskell

Personal recollections

[In the introduction of her biography of Elder S. N. Haskell, Ella M. Robinson shares recollections of those who had known him.]

I once asked the well-known radio preacher H. M. S. Richards if he had known Stephen Haskell.

"Yes, indeed," he replied, and related the following incident. "At a camp meeting in Waterloo, Quebec, in the year 1921, I mentioned that I needed more songbooks for an evangelistic effort I was conducting. S. N. Haskell, almost ninety years old, was present. He met me outside the tent, pulled out his pocketbook, and emptied . . . its entire contents into my hands. It amounted to a little more than seven dollars, and paid for several copies of *Christ in Song*.

"I remember Stephen Haskell as a deep and constant student of the Word of God," continued Elder Richards. "He hardly dared to take out his Bible while waiting . . . for a train, for fear he would become so absorbed in studying some line of truth that he would lose all contact with time. His train could come and go and he be left sitting there in the station still studying his Bible. . . ."

[In] my mind [I recall] a scene I once witnessed on the Avondale school estate in Australia. The elder, in overalls and rubber boots, was working with a group of students building a wooden bridge. He was a favorite leader of the work teams. No matter what the job, whether plowing or planting, building fences or draining land, he always found the best and easiest way of accomplishing it. Then, too, he was ever ready to enter into individual experiences and problems of students in an understanding and helpful manner.

Many people cherish memories regarding Elder Haskell. When Eugene Farnsworth was a lad in Washington, New Hampshire, some seventy miles[80] northwest of South Lancaster, Haskell, then in the prime of life, visited churches in that area. On one occasion, Farnsworth recalled, snow was deep and the weather extremely cold. "I remember seeing him pushing his way with his horse through the deep snowdrifts, visiting all the members. . . This was characteristic of this life and labors throughout the long years of his ministry."

A story is related demonstrating Elder Haskell's faith in God's personal guidance. While on a preaching tour in Georgia, Haskell felt impressed to leave the train unexpectedly at a deserted-looking station, explaining briefly to his secretary, a young man traveling with him, "Someone here needs help." The two were soon standing on the station platform with baggage piled beside them. There was not a soul in sight. They waited, praying silently.

Soon a car appeared. The driver greeted them. "Are you expecting someone to meet you?" he asked. "No," replied the elder, "but perhaps you can tell me if there are any Seventh-day Adventists in this part of the country?"

"Yes," replied the man. "An Adventist family lives about six miles from here. They operate a little school. I'll be glad to take you there."

The story continues: "Away they went with grateful hearts. Upon arriving, Elder Haskell remarked that he would go alone to the door of the house. After repeatedly knocking at the door he heard a faint voice inviting him in. As he entered he knew there was sickness in the home. The mother and her two daughters were ill, and the mother was quite discouraged. After a few kindly remarks and inquiries, Elder Haskell picked up the family Bible from the nearby table and read some of our heavenly Father's choice promises to the poor mother and daughters. Then came his warm and tender prayer for the sick ones, and heaven seemed nearer.

"He learned that the family conducted a self-supporting school for the neighborhood. Soon he saw children coming to the little schoolhouse close by and begin playing in their schoolyard, doubtless hoping their good teacher would be able that morning to teach. Elder Haskell gently advised the mother to let him send the children home, and tell them not to return for two weeks. This was done. The mother recovered quickly, also the girls, and after they had had a good rest, the school work was taken up again. Years later the mother told me that Elder Haskell's visit put new life into their hearts and into their work, and that they were never again discouraged over it."—**Ella M. Robinson, *S. N. Haskell, Man of Action*, 1967, pp. 8-10.**

Hearts electrified and aglow

[Elder Haskell] warned against the danger of working in a legalistic spirit without depending upon God; and he promised that, "with our hearts warm with the love of God, other hearts will become electrified and be aglow with the same spirit." He assured farmers that they need not be excluded from this soul-saving enterprise, and offered them some rather straight advice: If their large farms kept them at home, then let them sell off forty acres or so, and reduce their cares. He then made this stirring comment, "If the cause in which we are engaged means anything, it means everything; and to dabble with it at our fingers' ends, . . . look out first for ourselves and then give a little of our surplus time and means for the cause, is solemn mockery."—**ibid., pp. 37, 38.**

"God has offered no grander opportunity to those who would be His servants, and labor in His vineyard, than to go into a foreign country, there to educate the young, and instill into their minds pure and sound principles, which will fit them, not only for the practical duties of after life, but for a place of radiant brightness in the kingdom of God. . . ."—**ibid., p. 109.**

[Quotes from S. N. Haskell's articles in The True Missionary, *a short-lived journal published during 1874:]*

"It is when sacrifices that cost something are called for that the heart is tested."

"We should ask for great things and expect them."

"God is at work; and, work as fast as we may, his providence will keep ahead of us."

"The times call for action. . . . We have something else to attend to besides our farms and merchandise."

"The efforts we have made . . . [are] only a little field drill, testing the strength of our system, and learning how we can work together. Soon we shall be called upon to do something besides skirmish and drill."

"Love is an active principle, and cannot live without works. . . . The soil in which it grows is not the natural heart; but love is a heavenly plant, and flourishes only in a heart renewed by the grace of God."—**ibid., p. 41.**

Long and muddy roads

Haskell was a man of courage, endurance, and unbounded optimism. Neither weariness nor pain, bad roads nor poor transportation facilities, summer heat nor winter wind and snow—nothing! —dampened his spirits or abated his efforts. His persistent endeavors to meet all appointments, even under the most adverse conditions, were contagious. He wrote that at meetings where he expected only a small attendance or none at all, the brethren came in from different places, traveling all the way from ten to thirty-five miles.[81] He tells of one brother who walked twenty-five miles[82] so that his family might ride.

While he was visiting in New York State in January of 1876, when it was "neither sleighing nor wheeling," one brother, living fifty miles[83] away, started for the meeting on a stoneboat (a heavy sled used on the farm), came twenty-five miles, where he obtained a wagon, and brought another brother with him. Then he returned home and brought his family to Randolph, a distance of twenty-five miles,[84] where another meeting was held. Twenty-five miles was quite a journey without automobiles and along unpaved country roads where horses' feet and wagon wheels would sometimes sink deep in the mud.—**ibid., p. 42.**

Sharing your everything

In his Bible classes Elder Haskell took the book of Daniel verse by verse and dug into it with the purpose of getting all the meat there was in any particular scripture, using other portions of the Bible to help interpret difficult passages.

One day when he stated in class his belief that every portion of Scripture contained some valuable spiritual lesson, a student raised his hand. "I can't agree with that statement," he said; "I am sure that some portions of the Bible have a purely material significance."

"Will you give us an example?" asked the teacher. The young man stood up and read Paul's words to Timothy: " 'The cloak that I left at Troas with Carpus, when thou comest, bring with thee, and the books, but especially the parchments.' Now what spiritual lessons are we supposed to get out of that?"

Without hesitation Elder Haskell replied, "One of deep significance, especially for self-supporting workers in God's cause. The apostle Paul had brought the imperishable riches of heaven to thousands of souls; yet he was so poor in this world's goods that he preferred to wait an indefinite length of time while Timothy made the uncertain journey from Troas to Rome rather than to have money expended in purchasing a new coat and writing materials." He could say with a depth of experience known to but few, "as poor, yet making many rich; as having nothing, and yet possessing all things" (2 Cor. 6:10).

In the realm of personal sacrifice Haskell could speak from experience. Economical almost to a fault, he and Hetty were ever more careful of the Lord's money than of their own. It was not unusual for them to share their wages with others who were eager to do service for God, supporting them from their own meager allowance until the efforts of these new workers proved fruitful and their names were placed on the conference payroll.

Nor did the Haskells ever knowingly lose an opportunity to help a person in need. During their first year at Avondale, they had made room in their own home for a wayward child who had been expelled from school.

Elder Haskell remembered how he and his first wife, Mary, had worked for twenty years to own a home of their own. Just after securing a clear title to a house in South Lancaster, while still rejoicing that the mortgage was no more, they received word of a financial crisis in Battle Creek. Three thousand dollars was needed immediately. Uncomplainingly they remortgaged their property and sent the money to headquarters. Elder Haskell said afterward that although at the time it was a great trial to him, God had rewarded him ten times over in every sense of the word.—**ibid., pp. 150, 151.**

5

Anna Knight

Early Sabbath keeping

I decided to spend the day out in the woods, since there was no home I could go to and keep the Sabbath. When I had prepared breakfast for the family, which was my daily task, and had done my housework, I took my Bible, *Sabbath School Worker, Quarterly, Review and Herald, Instructor,* and my revolver, and went to the woods where I spent the day.

During the day I memorized the Sabbath school lesson and read the papers from cover to cover. My faithful dog in the meanwhile watched near by, never allowing a hog or cow to come near me. He did not bark, but quietly got up and drove them away should any come near. If it rained, I would go to the barn and spend the time in the hayloft.

Many hard things were said and even threats were made, but I let all know my mind was made up. When I went to the woods, I took my revolver; and I could shoot straight. The Lord did not permit any harm to befall me.—**Anna Knight,** *Mississippi Girl*, **p. 33,34, 1952.**

Kindness in a Sabbath dress

Mrs. Chambers[85] was a milliner and dressmaker and also a good baker. She had organized a group of women into a club called the "Women's Exchange." They had their wares in one of the leading grocery stores on Market Street. These ladies took turns and looked after their sales daily at this store. They cooked homemade whole-wheat bread, salt-rising bread, pies, cookies, and cakes, and also made needlework to sell.

Mrs. Chambers specialized in salt-rising bread, baking it about four days a week. She got up at four o'clock in the morning and stayed up until ten o'clock at night on bake days. Some days she would make sixty loaves, and her bakings were never less that thirty. I helped her all I could with her work. I carried the bread to the Exchange daily for her. I also learned how to make it, but she never would let me take the entire responsibility.

I learned that she was doing all this hard work to earn money to buy clothes for me to go to school. She did away with my old feathered hat and made me one suitable for a Seventh-day Adventist. She made me an outfit of clothing; and each time she would finish a garment, she would put it down carefully and say, "Anna, I hope this will last you until the Lord comes." I really tried to take good care of these clothes so that they would, but they did not last long. But the influence of her unselfish love and sacrifice is still living in my memory.

One day I was so overwhelmed by what she was doing for me, a poor colored girl and nothing at all to her except a member of her church, that I could not refrain from crying. I did not want her to see me, so I went up into the attic and had a big cry. She missed me. When she found me crying, she tenderly put her arms around me and asked, "Have you had bad news from home?"

"No."

"Are you homesick?"

"No."

"Have I hurt your feelings?"

"No."

"Then what is the matter?"

I told her I was thinking of all the nice things she had done and was doing for me, and that I was poor and had nothing and never would be able to pay her for all her goodness and kindness to me.

Then she hugged me close to her and, between laughing and crying, said, "You dear child, we don't expect any pay for what we are doing for you. We believe you will make a worker in God's cause some day; and if we should sleep before Christ comes, our work will go on through you. We have helped many girls get started in the Lord's work, and we are glad to be able to help you."

By that time I had dried my tears. When she began to cry, I thought I had better stop. I did not want to make her feel sad; however, I have since learned that hers were tears of joy, hoping that her labors would not be in vain.

That was in 1894, and from that day to this I have never forgotten her faith in me. I have tried to keep their work going on, since both she and her husband are sleeping in Jesus. I have never forgotten them or their faith in me. It has always been an inspiration to me and an incentive to help others.—**ibid., pp. 42-44.**

On a diet for India

There was a famine in India, and our own missionaries, some of whom were Battle Creek doctors and nurses, were facing a shortage of food.

Dr. Kellogg called all the doctors, nurses, and helpers together and told us of the cablegram which had been received, and appealed to us to make a sacrifice of *our food.* In other words, as he put it, go on a Hindu diet for one week, cut out everything from our board bill except those things which the sanitarium would not have to buy.

Then he placed the matter before us, asking for a show of hands by all those who would like to go on this special, restricted diet. Quite a large number, four or five hundred, raised their hands. Special tables were arranged, and at the end of a week we had saved $500. We liked it so well that we decided to carry on our sacrifice another week and were able to donate a $1,000 famine-relief fund from the saving on our board bill for two weeks. **—ibid., pp. 73, 74.**

School fees: $ 1.00 a month

Dr. Kellogg sent for me and a number of others who had gone out pioneering in missionary work. We were to come back to Battle Creek and take a postgraduate course. At the same time the sanitarium needed extra trained help to care for the large number of patients who were there during the summer.

I attended summer school at the college part of the time. There I got additional training to help me with my mission school in Mississippi.

When the postgraduate course was finished, each of us returned to her respective field of labor or to a new assignment. I went back to Mississippi to erect the new schoolhouse which I was planning to build.

The summer before, a friend of mine from Battle Creek, Miss Julia Luccock, who had been nursing a patient in Alabama, decided to visit her people and the camp meeting in Iowa. She stopped by to see me before going, planning to stay only a few days, but she was so interested in what I was trying to do that she spent nearly three weeks with me helping to plan the work. We drew a sketch of the building I wanted, and she took it with her to Iowa to show to her father and get suggestions from him, for he was a builder. She did this and returned it to me in due time with many helpful suggestions.

While at the camp meeting in Iowa, she solicited fifty dollars for the work and sent it to me by registered letter. I called a meeting of the patrons of the school and the friendly neighbors who were interested and willing to assist. I told them about my plans to build a schoolhouse and solicited their help. If they did not have money they could donate labor.

Everyone promised to do what he could. The men went to the woods, felled timber, and took old-fashioned broadaxes and hewed logs for the sills and sleepers. This was quite a saving on the lumber bill. We had split the boards for the roof before I left for Battle Creek some months before.

The women and children picked the cotton on my four acres,[86] and I sold it and put the money into the building fund.

When I made out the lumber bill and sent it to our little country sawmill, the owner of the mill was surprised, for this was the largest single order he had ever received at any one time. All the rough lumber such as framing, rafters, and joists I bought from him, but the finishing lumber for siding and window casings had to be bought in Ellisville twenty miles[87] away and brought out by mule team to the building plot. This was a big job which cost quite a sum of money. All the cotton money plus the fifty dollars from Miss Luccock, besides considerable advanced labor on tuition, was put into the building in addition to the free labor donations. In about eight weeks, by long hours of work and united effort, the building was completed.

I bought glass windows, a stove, and paint for blackboards. When the time came for school to open, we had the nicest schoolhouse anywhere in that section of the country. People came from as far as seventy-five miles[88] to see it.

I had twenty-four pupils in eight grades and a tuition charge for each pupil of one dollar a month. Only one patron was able to pay the tuition in cash each month. The others paid their tuition with part cash and part labor. The labor consisted of clearing an acre of land adjoining the school ground on which we planned to have an orchard and vineyard. I allowed the children part of their noon hour and after school for work sawing logs and wood from this ground. The logs were used to make rails to fence the vine-yard, and the wood was used in the stove.

I organized two Sunday schools, six miles[89] apart, and used *Our Little Friend* in each of them. One was held Sunday morning and the other in the afternoon. The Sabbath school children at Graysville, Tennessee, sent me their used papers which I would use first at one Sunday school and then at the other. Thus the same papers served three different places.

After the Sunday school lesson was over, I taught penman-ship, reading, and arithmetic to some adults who were unable to attend the regular day school. I also taught them better ways of cooking and how to can fruit, stressing especially the need of health and temperance among them.

The people were learning many things, but it was hard for them to see and accept all the message.—**ibid., pp. 80-83.**

6

Alma McKibbin

[Ellen White's counsel on elementary education during the mid-1890's exerted an extremely positive influence on Adventist education. During the decade from 1895 to 1905, the number of Adventist elementary schools grew from 18 to 417. It was in the midst of this phenomenal explosion in the number of Adventist church schools that pioneer California educator, Mrs. Alma McKibbin, authored our first elementary Bible textbooks.]

Twelve miles to the post office

Teachers were begging for Bible lessons. At summer schools some would sit for hours and copy lessons from my notebooks. At last Professor [M. E.] Cady[90] insisted that I have my lessons printed. Some teachers made no attempt to teach the Bible, because they had no prepared lessons. If the Bible was not taught, then all our effort to establish church schools was in vain.

And so once more I must do what I did not know how to do—write books and publish them. The Healdsburg College[91] Press printed my first books at my expense. The work went slowly. The college press was a very simple print shop, not too well equipped with anything, but the printer, Arthur Haines, did wonderfully well with his meager resources. I was not only author but proof-reader and business manager as well.

The teachers sent in orders and were so urgent that I could not wait for the entire book to be printed, but sent each signature as it came off the press. There were 12 signatures in the first book. Twelve times I trudged more than a mile[92] to the post office to mail them, doing this after my teaching day was done and home duties were yet to be done. Pioneer work is not easy.—**Alma E. McKibbin,** *Step by Step*, **1964, p. 80.**

The shoestring textbook

I'd begun in my first school to make outlines for these lessons, and right then, I had to make lessons for grades I was teaching. And these teachers wanted to know what I had taught in the family school and in this church school. All I had was my old battered notebooks in which I'd put the lessons, and written them on the board. They were just outlines, and somebody had said not to give lessons on Daniel, but to take the stories of the Old Testament. Well, I believe in chronology; I don't believe in teaching about Abraham before you teach about Adam. So I began with Adam. I made out my own lessons, and I'd advised these teachers to do that. But they came back to the next summer school. They'd gotten along very well with everything except Bible. They couldn't make lessons. They just couldn't do it! Well, Professor [M. E.] Cady says, "You'll have to publish yours." There was a press at the College, and they were printing whatever they needed in the College. He said they'll print your lessons for you. So I began the wearisome work. And in the first you know they'd print them by signatures. Well, they were in such haste for them that I punched holes in the signatures, and the only thing I had available was shoestring. I mailed a shoestring with the first one, put it through these holes, and told them other signatures would follow which they could add to it. And those were the first books. They called them "the shoestring books."

The next year the printer made backs for them. Then I gave them backs to put on, but before that they had nothing but a shoestring to hold these different signatures together. And then when they made the books, they made the holes to correspond, and that's the way they used the shoestrings. That's the way they were bound.—**McKibbin**, *oral history interview* **by James Nix, September 30, 1967.**

7

Percy T. Magan

Under a Maple tree

[Circumstances surrounding Magan's decision to decline W. K. Kellogg's offer to take charge of stock sales for his new cornflakes company]

Pioneering efforts are rarely easy and such was the case at the time Emmanuel Missionary College (now Andrews University) was relocated in Berrien Springs, Michigan, in 1901 from its former location in Battle Creek. It was a real struggle to get the fledgling institution established. Conditions were primitive. Classes were first held in twenty renovated former jail cells in the old abandoned court house. In fact, Dean Percy T. Magan found that his office had been the former county sheriff's! Students were lodged in a nearby hotel.

Besides attempting to build permanent buildings for the school, the administrators of the institution were also trying to carry out reforms in the curriculum. Students were expected to work as part of the program. Because it was a missionary school, the Bible was to be central to each class and degrees were not granted when one graduated. Some on the board felt that the reforms were being carried too far.

Matters came to a head in 1904. Both Dean Magan and President Edward A. Sutherland[93] resigned. Less than a week earlier, Percy Magan's wife[94] had died. Though the two men were re-elected by the board, the situation was such that a short time later they both resigned again and went south where they started Madison College in Tennessee.

In 1930 Dr. Magan wrote to Elder William A. Spicer[95] who was president of the General Conference at the time. Now, early in the depression and over a quarter of a century after that eventful time back in 1904, Magan wrote to his longtime friend:

"I often think of the times when my first wife died at Berrien Springs in 1904. . . . W. K. [Kellogg][96] came to me. . . and begged me to quit work and join him in the cornflakes company which at that moment was in the process of organization. He offered me a block of stock, ten thousand dollars worth at par value. He wanted me to take charge of stock sales and offered me a commission on all I sold with a permanent place in the company when this work was done. That ten thousand dollars of stock would be worth today somewhere in the neighborhood of one million dollars, and of course trading on that I could have made it probably three or four million. The offer in a way was tempting. But I remember well spending the greater part of a night under a maple tree at old Berrien, then in the process of its own birth, and talking the whole matter over with the Master. And as the morning light broke I had decided it that in spite of all difficulties with brethren I must stick to this Message and give whatever time and talent I had to the making of Adventists rather than to the making of cornflakes. [P. T. Magan letter to W. A. Spicer, April 21, 1930, p. 3.]—**Paul A. Gordon and James R. Nix,** *Laughter and Tears of the Pioneers,* **1989, pp. 26, 27.**

8

John G. Matteson

Preacher and typesetter

In the 1860's, when Elder Matteson was preaching among the Scandinavian people in the United States, he felt so keenly the need of literature in their own languages that he went into the *Review* office and himself set type for our first Swedish tracts. —**Ella M. Robinson,** ***Man of Action,*** **pp. 45, 46.**

9

Washington Morse

Walking hundreds of miles

In the years 1857, 1858, and 1859, I walked hundreds of miles in Minnesota, visiting the widely scattered settlements, carrying my Bible, chart, and tracts, endeavoring to awaken an interest in the truths of the third angel's message. Quite a goodly number of worthy people embraced the truth as the result of the labors so bestowed, although they were put forth in much weakness, and under unfavorable conditions. . . . The *first* S. D. Adventists to settle in Minnesota, to the best of my knowledge, were a sister Green (now living at Hebron, Wis.) and her father. Although a distance of from thirty to eighty miles[97] separated those few families of like precious faith, they did not deem it a very severe task to get together for an occasional meeting, notwithstanding an ox team and farm wagon constituted the only mode of conveyance, with some of them at least. —**Washington Morse, "Items of Advent Experience During the Past Fifty Years.-No. 6,"** *Review and Herald*, **November 6, 1888, pp. 689, 690.**

10

William A. Spicer

No posts of honor

[Spicer served as secretary of the General Conference from 1903 to 1922. Although the two following stories both happened after 1915, they are so characteristic of this church leader that they are included in this collection. Hoping to retire as General Conference Secretary in 1922 in favor of some lesser position, Spicer, in spite of trying his best to get out of it, found himself elected as the new General Conference president. When the delegates had deadlocked over whether or not to reelect Elder A. G. Daniells,[98] who already had been president since 1901, they finally turned to Elder Spicer. After several suggestions of other possible candidates, none of whom were satisfactory to the delegates, Spicer finally agreed to serve. It is in this context that he wrote the following to his wife, "Georgie," who had not accompanied her husband to the General Conference Session. The last phrase succinctly summarizes Elder Spicer's philosophy of service, and explains why the delegates wanted him to be their new president.]

I begged all to try to think of some other way, but after a season of prayer no way seemed open [and] I could not refuse. I am sorry for you dear Georgie. You would not wish it for me. It is so different from the work I longed to do. But I just couldn't get out of it without selfishness. Don't worry. It does not call for a superman but just for a consecrated man doing his best, and that I will be, Georgie dear, by God's help. Don't worry, Dear Georgie, four years and I will have my successor ready, you may be sure.[99] So dear sweet wife I am just your husband that loves you and would rather have the Kingdom of your heart than any office honors. There are no posts of honor but only of service.—**W. A. Spicer, letter to his wife, Georgie, written from San Francisco, California, May 22, 1922.**

Steward of the Lord's Money

[Another post-1915 story about Elder Spicer, but, again, one that demonstrates his willingness to sacrifice for the message in which he so much believed.]

One time, when visiting the Ellen G. White Estate while working as director of their Research Center at Loma Linda University, I stayed as a guest in Arthur and Frieda White's small cottage adjacent to their home in Adelphi, Maryland. While reminiscing with me about the past, Elder White told me about something that happened to him on the way back to Takoma Park, Maryland, following the first Fall Council he attended after becoming Secretary of the Ellen G. White Estate.

It seems that on more than one occasion, Dr. J. H. Kellogg invited his former fellow Adventist church leaders to hold Fall Council at the Battle Creek Sanitarium. Whether enough time had passed so the doctor actually felt comfortable in doing this, or it was just the fact that he desperately needed money for his sanitarium, I do not know. Anyway, Fall Council that year (presumably 1938, from the circumstances Elder White described) was held at the Battle Creek Sanitarium.

After the meetings had concluded, Elder White and many of the other church leaders took the train back to Takoma Park. As Elder White said to me, "Having grown up in the White family, I was used to making sacrifices for the cause, so to save money, I got an upper berth in one of the sleepers for the overnight trip back to Washington. Upper berths were cheaper than lower berths, so I felt I was saving the Lord's cause some money by getting an upper one."

Sometime during the course of that overnight train trip, Elder White decided to stretch his legs a bit, so started walking through the train. Coming into one of the coaches, whom should he see but Elder W. A. Spicer, sitting in one of the seats with a blanket pulled up around his shoulders. Elder White told me that he had never felt so humiliated in all his life. There was old Elder Spicer, a man more than twice Arthur White's age, who would not even think of spending enough of the Lord's money to get an upper sleeping berth for the overnight train trip back home. Instead, Elder Spicer chose to sit up overnight on the train rather than spend the money on his own personal comfort. Why? Because the funds saved would then be available to help further spread the Advent message. With Elder Spicer, and many of our Adventist pioneers, there was nothing unusual about this type of reasoning; that was their way of life. Of course, Elder Spicer said nothing about all this to Arthur White. But Elder White told me that on that train trip, Elder Spicer's quiet witness taught him a powerful lesson regarding real commitment and sacrifice when it comes to spreading the Advent message.—**Arthur L. White, Story about W. A. Spicer told to James R. Nix in the late 1970's.**

11

R. A. Underwood

Privacy in cotton sheets

At this time the office of both the conference and the tract society was located in my home at Mesopotamia, Ohio. We had dedicated the best room in the house to this purpose, and the fuel, the rent, and all the work of the office were freely given by my wife and myself to the Ohio Conference. Not only were the books kept by my wife, but a large correspondence was carried on with the churches and scattered believers. The conference was thus enabled to take on one or two ministers for field work. I also was giving my time largely to the conference. Thus it was necessary for us to employ help to do our housework and operate the farm. I mention these experiences that we may get a glimpse of the past, and not forget the struggles and sacrifices of those earlier days. . . .

The first remuneration I received from the conference was $4 a week. My wife and I studied economy in every way possible. As an example, while I was president of the Ohio and Pennsylvania Conferences, which covered a period of fourteen years, it was my custom in visiting churches to arrange to make a circuit, visiting from eight to twelve churches on one trip, to save time and railway fare. I would often be away from home for two, three, or four months.

My correspondence was done in the old-fashioned way, with pen, the tablet usually resting on my knee while I wrote. Stenographers and typewriters were unknown in those early days. . . .

My first experience in riding in a railroad sleeper was early in the eighties. The General Conference had recommended that Elder E. W. Farnsworth and I visit California, and spend several months in general labor in that State. The Union Pacific Railroad had just installed a tourists' sleeper service from Chicago to San Francisco, the bed being simply narrow wood slats, without mattress or bedding. Before boarding the train in Chicago, we secured straw ticks and bedding for our berths. With extra cotton sheets we screened ourselves from the gaze of others in the car. However antiquated this method may now seem, it was a great improvement over sitting up for five or six nights. The railroad charge for the sleeper was $3 for the trip. I was about fifty years old before I ever rode in an upholstered sleeper, although as a member of the General Conference Committee I often rode two or more days on the train to reach a camp-meeting or other important gathering.—**R. A. Underwood, "Reminiscences and Early Experiences,"** *Review and Herald*, **September 18, 1924, pp. 55, 56.**

12

James and Ellen White

Tobacco smoke and carpet-bag pillows

For lack of means, we took the cheapest private conveyance, second-class cars, and lower-deck passage on steamships. Private conveyance was the most comfortable for Mrs. White, who was feeble. I could then endure hardships, labors and privations to almost any extent for the sake of the truth of God and his precious, scattered people. When in second-class cars we were usually enveloped in tobacco smoke. This I could endure, but Mrs. White would frequently faint. When on steamers, on the lower deck, we suffered the same from the smoke of tobacco, besides the swearing and vulgar conversation of the ship hands and the baser portion of the traveling public. Sleeping conveniences are summed up as follows: We lay down on the hard floor, dry-goods boxes, or sacks of grain, with carpetbags for pillows, without covering except overcoats or shawls. If suffering from the winter cold, we would walk the deck to keep warm. If suffering from the heat of summer, we would go on the upper deck to get the cool night air. This was fatiguing to Mrs. White, especially with an infant in her arms.—**Review and Herald, August 2, 1923, p. 66.**

Stocking full of coins to the rescue

James White was troubled as he walked slowly up the path, climbed the stairs and entered his Rochester home.[100] He found Ellen busily sewing in the bedroom. Wearily he sank onto a chair. Ellen could see that something was troubling him. "What is it, James? What is wrong?"

"It's time to bring out another issue of the *Review*, but we have hardly any paper and no money with which to pay for the shipment that has come."

"How much money do you need?" she asked.

"Sixty-four dollars," he replied, "but it might as well be $10,000."

Ellen rose and walked to the closet. She opened the door, reached in, grasped a black stocking hanging from a nail, brought it out and placed it in her husband's hands.

"What is this?" he asked, although he could feel coins inside the stocking. He tipped it up and a cascade of half dollars, quarters, dimes, and nickels[101] poured out.

"Wherever did you get all this?" he asked in amazement.

"I've always believed a person should save something for a rainy day," Ellen answered. "For months I have been saving as much as I could. I hope it's enough."

James counted the coins. It was enough! Through his wife's foresight a crisis was averted, and he was able to take delivery of the necessary paper.—**Robinson, *James White*, p. 105.**

Everything I have belongs to God

[In 1861 James White gave the newly-incorporated Seventh-day Adventist Publishing Association all the assets that he had developed for the publishing work since its founding.]

Elder [James] White . . . stated . . . : "When, in 1861, the publishing association was instituted at Battle Creek, Mich., we gave our list of subscribers and the right to publish all our works (since decided to have been worth $10,000) to the association." Of this act Sister White, in Volume III of the "Testimonies," page 87, thus speaks, "After he had spent years of his life in privation and unceasing toil to establish the publishing interests upon a sure basis, he gave away to the people of God that which was his own."—**J. N. Loughborough, "Second Advent Experience-No. 7,"** *Review and Herald*, **July 26, 1923, p. 5.**

[In 1875, James White supported, from his own funds, the founding of the Pacific Press Publishing Company in Oakland, California.]

In February, 1875, James and Ellen White, accompanied by J. H. Waggoner, . . . returned to the state [of California]. On the twelfth of that month a special session of the California Conference was called in Oakland to consider a building site for the new enterprise;[102] and after prayerful consideration they selected a lot 80 x 100 feet[103] on Castro Street between Eleventh and Twelfth.

On April 1, 1875, the Pacific Seventh-day Adventist Publishing Association was organized; and O. B. Jones of Battle Creek, Michigan, builder of the Review and Herald offices, began the construction of the new plant. It was in the form of a Greek cross, 66 x 26[104] east and west, by 46 x 26[105] north and south. James White was soon on his way to New York to purchase equipment. He also disposed of some personal property in the East in order to aid in financing the venture, for at that time not all the pledges had been paid. At a personal expense of $650 he brought five trained young people from the East to work with him. He had already contributed in the amount of $1,000 to the publishing fund.—**Harold O. McCumber,** *Pioneering the Message in the Golden West*, **1968 ed., pp. 103, 104.**

Between the eastern and western camp meetings, the Whites stayed with friends in Battle Creek. When word came that the new building in Oakland was nearing completion, James traveled to New York to purchase equipment for it. Since some of the pledges made at Yountville[106] had not been redeemed, he found it necessary to sell both his properties in Battle Creek in order to raise funds to buy a press. The equipment he purchased cost about $10,000.

Sacrifices by the Whites such as they made on this occasion were not uncommon. Many times in the past they had felt compelled to act similarly.—**Robinson, *White*, p. 255.**

Free room and board for God's workers

"Be not forgetful to entertain strangers" (Heb. 13:2). All their lives, James and Ellen White would practice that injunction. No one was ever turned hungry from their door. Whatever they had they gladly shared. Both were generous-hearted, far beyond the average.

While Elder White was living in Greenville [Michigan] he heard that a woman named Hannah More had recently come to Battle Creek from New England in search of employment. Sister Moore had spend many years as a missionary in Central Africa working for another denomination. Someone had placed in her hands a copy of J. N. Andrews' book *The History of the Sabbath* while she was on furlough. She read it and after her return to Central Africa began to observe the seventh-day Sabbath. As a result, she was dismissed by her mission society and returned to the United States.

She lived in South Lancaster, Massachusetts, for a time, then went to Battle Creek, hoping to find employment there. She was not successful and, finding no door open to receive her, accepted the invitation of a non-Adventist friend, a Mr. Thompson, who had also been a missionary, to go to his home in northern Michigan and teach his children.

When James heard of the cool, indifferent way the church members in Battle Creek had treated Miss More, he felt ashamed of them. He promptly wrote, inviting her to return and make her home with him and Ellen in Greenville. Miss More replied that she had spent all her money making the trip to her present residence. She would come when she had earned the fare, for she was eager to meet the Whites.

James replied that he and Ellen were leaving for New England to hold meetings, but when they returned in two months they would certainly send money so she could come and live with them. Unfortunately, their trip lasted nearly four months, and by the time they returned to Michigan, winter had its grip on the land, and Miss More could not travel.

Before the next spring came, Hannah More died and was buried in northern Michigan. James and Ellen grieved deeply. They were convinced that her life might have been saved if some interest had been taken in her when she passed through Battle Creek. [*Testimonies*, vol. 1, pp. 666-680.]

At the time of general meetings in Battle Creek, many old friends were entertained at the White home. On one occasion as many as thirty-five persons sat down to eat at their table, all at the expense of the generous host and hostess. There were no entertainment allowances in the 1860's.

One habit James White practiced was that of donating his own clothing to help others. The first time we read of this was in Vermont, where the Whites had gone to attend a conference. James met a brother identified simply as N. A. H. James learned that this man was extremely poor and from his own meager purse he took twenty dollars, which he handed to this brother. But he went still further. He took off his own overcoat, the only one he had, and handed it to N. A. H. The act is even more impressive when we learn that this same brother had aroused an attitude of jealousy in others toward Elder White. [*Life Sketches* (1880), p. 279.]

J. O. Corliss was one of a number of young preachers whom James and Ellen White took into their home to help train for work in the cause of God. This young man lived with them for two years. Concerning James White's generosity to the poor, Corliss reported:

"Elder White was very tender-hearted toward cases of need.

I have seen him give no less than three overcoats in a single winter to poor preachers needing such garments. More than that, when he thought some hard-working messenger was being scantily dealt with by an auditing committee, he was not slow to appear before that board of award, to champion the misused one's cause, and always to good effect." [J. O. Corliss, in Advent Review and Sabbath Herald, Aug. 23, 1923.]

It should be noted that James, who had scant sympathy for drones, did this on behalf of the "hard-working messenger."

Young workers who received such generous treatment at the hands of Elder White never forgot his kindness. Ten years after the death of his benefactor, L. R. Conradi wrote to Ellen White:

"It was my privilege to make you and your dear husband's acquaintance shortly after embracing the truth {1878} and I shall never forget his kindness, as he bought me a coat in which I graduated and gave me the charts when I began to preach." [L. R. Conradi letter to Ellen G. White, Aug. 16, 1891.]

That there might be money on hand when some worker faced an emergency or a church member needed immediate help, Elder White suggested the setting up of a fund for this purpose. Money was collected, and the first Benevolent Society was established, an organization that flourished for many years. Many worthy individuals had cause to bless Elder White for his part in the establishment of this society.

In those days there were many calls for the support of new enterprises. There was a book fund used for translating Adventist publications into foreign languages. The Health Reform Institute and the Review and Herald Publishing Association always needed more capital, and after 1874 there was the overseas European Mission needing help, as well as Battle Creek College.

The back of the *Review* carried many lists of persons who were contributing to these and other worthy causes. In those columns, Elder White called for "fifty-dollar men" and "hundred-dollar men," and before he died, he was asking for a number of "thousand-dollar men." The names of James and Ellen White headed nearly every list. This fact was acknowledged by the General Conference Committee:

"Elder White . . . sold his property in Michigan and Iowa at a sacrifice in 1875, and is prepared to show that he has donated more than $5,000 to the cause during the past two years. . . .

"These very grumblers do little or nothing for the cause themselves, while Elder White at the same time is giving a hundred here, and a thousand there. He pledges himself to give to the cause during the year 1876 more than all these murmurers put together from the Atlantic to the Pacific." [Administrative Pamphlets: *Danger and Duties of Our Time*, General Conference Committee, pp. 42, 46, 47.]

James White, like Job of old, sought out the cases of the poor and the needy. In 1874 drought and grasshoppers devastated Kansas, reducing many farmers to penury. Wages of Adventist workers in that State were so reduced that they could not live on what they received. Hearing of this, Elder White protested that men could not feed their families on the low wages they were receiving. He promptly launched a fund for the relief of the Kansas workers. His and Ellen's generous donation of $100 headed the list. Workers in Kansas were deeply grateful. [*Review and Herald*, Nov. 4, 1875.]

On several occasions James paid interest on money he borrowed from the bank to lend, interest free, to workers so they could purchase homes for their families. Among others helped in this way were Elders Loughborough, Mead, Waggoner, and Hull. [*Defense of Eld. James White and Wife*, (Battle Creek. Michigan, 1870), pp. 19, 20.]

When the cause of God prospered, James White rejoiced. When he saw excellent results obtained by Adventist preachers with gospel tents, James urged one conference after another to invest in them. For his own beloved Michigan, he purchased a tent costing more than five hundred dollars. This tent he was willing to lend to any minister who could use it for evangelistic meetings. [James White, in *Review and Herald*, June 8, 1869.]

In 1878 a heavy debt hung over the church in Oakland, California, and there was real danger that through bankruptcy it might be taken from the believers. Edson White, in California at the time, wrote to his parents, asking, Shall the church be sold to the 'Campbellites" (who wanted to buy the building). Mrs. White said No, and James White said No. Sooner than allow that to happen, James indicated that he would sell his house in Oakland. [*Ibid.*][107]

Ellen's plan was somewhat different: "Let there be a Christmas tree in every church in California, to be covered all over with fruit in the form of cash, in sums all the way from a dime to one hundred dollars." [*Ibid.*][108]

At the same time she asked Edson to place $100 on the tree from James and the same amount from herself. She wrote to her other son, Willie, who was in Battle Creek, instructing him to place similar sums on a Christmas tree to be set up in the "Dime Tabernacle."

At the time of the death of White, in 1881, George I. Butler, General Conference president, referred to the generosity of the fallen leader:

"There was a tender place in his heart toward the distressed and those whom he thought were wronged, which made him one of the most generous of men. How many there are among us who have been helped and encouraged by his means, his words, and his acts. How many times he has hurried away from busy cares to pray with the sick and sorrowing. Not every one who knew him was aware of the peculiar tenderness of heart which he really possessed, or gave him credit for this trait of character; but his most intimate friends know that I state the truth. I never knew a man who could more generously forgive a wrong when he thought it was truly repented of than he." [George I. Butler in *Review and Herald*, Aug. 16, 1881.]

During the years, James White enjoyed the blessing promised to the openhanded, proving the truthfulness of the statement, "The liberal soul shall be made fat: and he that watereth shall be watered also himself" (Prov. 11:25).

Uriah Smith, reporting in the *Review*, stated, on Elder White's funeral, "Memory brushes the dimness, accumulating through the lapse of time, from numberless deeds of kindness received at his hand." [Uriah Smith, in *Review and Herald*, Aug. 16, 1881.] —Robinson, *White*, pp. 214-218.

Never mind if the house burned down

This is how we got our means; as God saw the use we made of the means He gave us, He intrusted us with more. My husband was a financier. I made the statement last night that we had invested $30,000 in the cause, and this is the way we have done it—when we saw a place where the cause needed means, we would hand it out.

When we went over to the Pacific Coast, many were raised up to obey God, and then we wanted means to build a meeting-house; but the people were poor, so we sent over to Michigan, telling them to sell all that we had, and there we invested our means, and a meetinghouse was built in San Francisco and Oakland. Often when returning from a long journey we would look to see if our house had burned down in our absence. And my husband would say, "Never mind if the house does burn, we have a treasure laid up in heaven."

Now I cannot afford to use my means for my own glory, I want it invested to God's glory. When the mission started in Basel, the word came, We must have means. I had received from a sister a silk dress; This I sold, and sent $50.00 to help the mission. And when my good sisters knew what I had done, they followed my example, and the sum was made up. Instead of putting my means on my own body, I would rather it would go to the widow and fatherless to clothe them. And now the reason we have been able to deposit this in God's treasury is because of the benevolence of

God; and yet we have some little property left. And since I have seen the missions in such great need, my letters have gone to Healdsburg, California, telling them to sell my house and furniture and send the means over that I can dispose of it to help these missions.

This is the way we have been working ever since we have had a part in this work. I want you to understand that because God has given us means, . . . we have tried to use it to His glory. I do not feel that anything I have is my own, and when I go to the store to buy anything, I question, Cannot I do without this and put the money into the cause? I repeat it again and again to myself, "Jesus for my sake became poor. He had not where to lay His head; and then shall I who am the subject of His grace have a better time than He?"—*Manuscript Releases*, vol. 19, pp. 137, 138.

We have tried to the best of our ability to save means in every way possible, that the work of God might go forward. I had about the time of Bro. Ertzenberger's visit to America a present of a nice silk dress, which cost forty-five dollars. Brother Andrews had just sent word that there was a great need of money to carry forward the work. I thought it was my privilege to so use the gift I had received that those who generously presented it to me would receive a reward and lay up treasure in heaven. I went to a merchant and told him to sell it for me for all he could get. He sold it for fifty dollars, and I sent the money to this mission. When others knew what I had done, they donated much larger sums. Thus the act of my doing this little, brought in means from other individuals, so that Brother Andrews wrote us that the very sum needed came at the right time, and he expressed gratitude to God for this timely response. . . .

We are establishing missions and building churches all through America. Already we have $23,000 laid up in the bank of heaven. As I could not sell property that I wished to sell, I have hired money and, paying eight percent interest, invested it in the cause. Our foreign mission treasury is now empty. In many places in America they have been having very close times. A night before last, I dreamed that I was pleading with God and presenting to Him our empty treasury. I awoke myself, pleading that He would send means to advance His work. Now I propose that we have living faith to ask God to supply our needs. The Lord has money that He has entrusted to His stewards for to do this needed work. Are these men, are these women where God can impress them with His Spirit?

A short time ago we wanted so much to build a boarding house in Healdsburg, California, to be connected with the school there. But we had no means to do it with. I said to my son, All we can do is to pray. We did pray. Our supplication went up to heaven with many tears for the Lord (to) send us means. In about three hours' time, I heard a knock at my door. Upon opening it, I found a sister there. Said she, I do not wish to disturb you while writing, but I have some money that I want to invest in the cause. Can you tell me where this money is most needed? Where shall it be placed? My heart was filled with gratitude to God. Yes, indeed, we had a place for it. She gave us (to the college) $5,000, enough to supply our present needs, and said she felt thankful that she could help the cause of God in any way. And the tears ran down her face to think that she had now found a safe deposit for what had so long been only a source of care and anxiety. There are others who should see and feel the needs of God's cause and do likewise. Why cannot we carry these things to God in prayer? We depend too much upon one another and too little upon God.—**Manuscript 19, 1885 (Ellen G. White manuscript written in Basel, Switzerland, Sept. 21, 1885).**

The 60 Pounds[109] that went to Sister Caro to help bear the load she was carrying, I meant to invest in the meeting-house in Melbourne; but there seems to be more than six ways to expend every shilling[110] in the work that needs to be done. It seems very hard to arouse our brethren to understand the wants of the cause of God in this new field. I have made my decision that no money from me will any more be expended in sending persons to Battle Creek, or supporting their tuition in Battle Creek. Those who can have a few months' advantages of school here shall have it.

Already I have paid above one thousand dollars, and nearly all of this is engaged in missionary work. I paid three hundred dollars to send a poor afflicted brother to St. Helena for treatment. He had contracted rheumatism on board the <u>Pitcairn</u>, and in laboring in damp districts received no help, and returned a great sufferer. I paid the expenses of Sister Miller to Oakland, that her husband might go into the office in Oakland, and become more efficient in some branches of the work here in the Echo Office.

Thus I have tried to work, investing in two meetinghouses, one hundred dollars in one, and one hundred and fifty in another; in four other meetinghouses, five pounds[111] each. Meetinghouses must be erected in the places where churches are raised up. A hall has been secured in Ashfield. All the opposition of five ministers has been set in operation to stop the work, and the last thing before leaving Granville, Brother McCullagh read a notice that they could not rent the hall any longer to Seventh-day Adventists. In two weeks' time the hall must be vacated by them. No other hall can be secured. We have purchased a new tent, to be erected in Canterbury, a new location, to lift the standard of truth. Five pounds I donated to this enterprise. But I shall continue to invest as long as I can command any means, that the cause of God shall not languish.—**Letter 46, 1895 (Ellen G. White letter to Dr. J. H. Kellogg written April 15, 1895).**

I do not profess to be the owner of any money that comes into my hands.—**Letter 46a, 1894, (Ellen G. White letter to Dr. J. H. Kellogg written October 25, 1894).**

Sometimes it has been reported that I am trying to get rich. Some have written to us, inquiring, "Is not Mrs. White worth millions of dollars?" I am glad that I can say, "No." I do not own in this world any place that is free from debt. Why?—Because I see so much missionary work to be done. Under such circumstances, could I hoard money?—No, indeed, I receive royalties from the sale of my books; but nearly all is spent in missionary work.

The head of one of our publishing houses in a distant foreign land, upon hearing from others recently that I was in need of means, sent me a bill of exchange for five hundred dollars; and in the letter accompanying the money, he said that in return for the thousands upon thousands of dollars royalty that I had turned over to their mission field for the translation and distribution of new books and for the support of new missionary enterprises, they regarded the enclosed five hundred dollars as a very small token of their appreciation. They sent this because of their desire to help me in my time of special need; but heretofore I have given, for the support of the Lord's cause in foreign lands, all the royalties that come from the sale of my foreign books in Europe; and I intend to return this five hundred dollars as soon as I can free myself from debt.—**Ellen G. White,** *Selected Messages,* **bk 1, 1958, p. 103.**

Royalties for God and His people

When she began to write, her royalties, of course, were quite small. Gradually they increased, but they were used up as fast as they came in, and faster. Sometimes she had to mortgage them into the future to meet the expenses of translating and illustrating. Often our young publishing houses were unable to meet this expense. She realized how greatly the books were needed.

There were other places where Ellen G. White felt urgent need for her money. Thousands of dollars went into the education of young people. Other thousands were contributed towards the erection of church buildings, and schools, and sanitariums. At times she even borrowed money and paid interest on it in order to take advantage of unusual opportunities to obtain valuable properties that were needed for the advancement of the cause.

It was unthinkable for Grandma to refuse any appeal for means if it were possible for her to give it. I[112] well remember a conversation through a half-open door of her writing room. Elder S. N. Haskell was appealing to her for five hundred dollars to assist in the erection of a church building in an unprosperous locality. She listened to his plea and then sent for Miss Sara Peck, who was acting temporarily as bookkeeper. "Sara," she said, "I want you to go carefully over my account and see if you can find any of my book royalties that haven't been mortgaged into the future. If so, let Elder Haskell have his five hundred dollars." . . . It must have been so, judging from the smile on his face when he came to our house to say good-bye.

One remark that I heard grandmother make during this conversation with Elder Haskell, I still remember. Even after sixty years I can hear the pathos in her voice as she said, "Oh, Elder Haskell, if there's anything I can do to help poor sinners find their way to Christ, that is what I want to do."

Throughout her life, Grandma did much to help the poor and unfortunate. I remember in Australia while going with her to woolen mills. She would purchase good, woolen material at wholesale prices, bring it home, and lay it away in a drawer in her room. While speaking on the Sabbath she might see a poorly dressed sister in the audience. She would make it a point to speak to her after the services, and invite her to her home during the week. While in conversation, Grandma might say something like this, "I was fortunate in coming into possession of a nice piece of material that I think would be very becoming to you." She would then bring out the pieces for this sister. "If you have no objections I should like to have my seamstress to make it up for you."

Grandma's liberality demanded the strictest personal economy. One day Mrs. George B. Starr was visiting at Sunnyside;[113] it happened to be wash day. Sister Starr, noticing an unusually patched piece of underwear hanging on the line, exclaimed, "Oh, Sister White, you ought not to have to wear such things. Put it in the Dorcas barrel, and I'll get you some new ones." "No," replied Grandma, "I never give my old things to poor folks. It might discourage them. Poor people often have poor ways and let things go to pieces. But I know how to mend and patch." And she did.

If she saw Mabel[114] or me with a tear in the dress we had on, she would ask us to stand beside her, and watch as she mended it so we could do it ourselves the next time. And when she finished, you would have thought a tailor had done the mending, so carefully were the stitches taken.

No rag carpets in heaven

Especially in her early days did she have to put economy to a stretch. She encouraged her friends to bring their [old] clothes to her. She'd look them over carefully and select the least worn parts. These she would cut into strips and wind into balls and then braid them. Out of them she made her rugs and carpets. One day as she was working among the carpet rags, her husband, James, entered the room. Seeing the litter strewn all over the floor, he began singing,

"There'll be no rag carpets in heaven;

In that land of love,

In the heaven above,

There'll be no rag carpets in heaven."

Grandma had to put her carpet rags away, out of sight. She probably got our her knitting. Every moment was precious.

Save the bottle, save the cork

Many stories are told about her economy in the early days of poverty. One time while traveling on the train, they had, as usual, finished eating out of their lunch basket. James picked up an empty bottle, opened the car window, and was about to throw it out. "Don't throw that bottle away; it's useful," said Grandma. "Ellen, how can we lug such things around with us wherever we go?" Out went the bottle. His wife looked woefully after it and said in a mournful tone, "Oh, James, you might have saved the cork!"
—Ella M. (White) Robinson, oral history interview with James R. Nix, July 25, 1967, transcript pp. 16-19.

Section V

CONVERSIONS IN THE SOUTH

1

A Church for Slaves

A church had to be built at once.[115] Among black people even in slavery days the church was the major social institution. Having a church building in which to meet was understandably of deep importance to them. Thus, when these new Adventists were taunted by friends, "You have no church, and these missionaries will go away pretty soon. Then where will you be?" the words cut.

Edson and Will Palmer had very little money, and their newly acquired parishioners had even less, but since they had assurance from the Lord that the way would be opened, they laid plans for a church.

They decided on a building 20 x 40[116] feet which would cost $100 and made arrangements to pay for the lumber in installments. With much difficulty Palmer and White managed to obtain a $2 a month lease on a lot on the corner of Walnut and First East streets.

After two days of vigorous building, the missionaries realized that they had failed to secure a building permit. Will Palmer, sent off to find the proper consent, located the man in charge of issuing building permits, and discovered that he was also the alderman for the ward in which the church was being built.

"What is this building to be used for?" the man asked.

"We will use it as a church and a schoolhouse for our work among the Negro people," replied Palmer.

The alderman's face clouded. "Well," he growled, "you might as well forget about it. I'm not going to have any midnight meetings with all that shouting in my neighborhood. If that church is for colored folk, I'll fight it as long as I live." Construction stopped.

The small company began praying that a way would be worked out for them to continue. For ten days they prayed. No results. Finally, Palmer went back to see the alderman.

He begged, pleaded, explained, and talked until the alderman, probably thinking he had found an easy way to evade the issue, agreed to a deal: "You get two people who own property near that church to sign a paper saying it's all right to build," he said, "and I'll let you."

For two days White and Palmer went from house to house. Palmer would go to the door to explain their mission while White would stay in the street and pray. They got the signatures and were soon back on the job.

In a letter to the General Conference Secretary, Leroy Nicola, Edson tells how the church was paid for.

"Bro. Palmer and I have each given $10. Sister Osborne, the Baptist missionary whom we found here when we came (and who has accepted the truth intelligently on all points), gave $5. This covers one-fourth of the first cost of the material, but the balance will be a millstone unless there is help for this poor people. They are willing, but every dollar they give means to go without shoes or clothing or proper food. That is sacrifice, and yet all have bravely come up and are doing their level best.

"We had a meeting at my house last evening after the Sabbath to consider the work, and the anxiety and desire to do on the part of these poor people were almost more than I could endure. For I knew every one of them, and the sacrifice that every cent given for this their church meant to them. Some of them hardly see 50 cents cash a week, and some have been kept from the meetings on account of being absolutely without shoes to wear. Others I have helped to get food to eat when I knew their cupboards were empty—and yet they all want an interest in their church.

"If this is not making a covenant with the Lord by sacrifice I do not know where it comes in. Women who have had to come to me for the loan of a little money to enable them to pay the rent of a little spot of ground on which their cabin is located, pledged themselves to assist in this enterprise, but in this way—'I want a part in this work, and will do all I can, but cannot say now what it will be.' Of course not. They will have to pinch here, and cut there, and shave in another place, and by and by they will be able to give, some 25 cents, some 50 cents, and perhaps in rare cases $1.

"And right here I want to say that I never saw a firmer body of Seventh-day Adventists than the little colored company in Vicksburg."

The weather was so hot while they were building that unless the nails were kept covered, they were impossible to handle. Edson wrote that "This is a terrible time to remain in the South," and asked L. T. Nicola if he couldn't get a job in Battle Creek for a few months.

Money became more and more scarce. At one point during construction Edson wrote to Battle Creek that he had only eighty cents for food the next week. But he said, "We shall see this church through if we have to live on cornmeal mush and water."

As the church neared completion, Edson was proud to announce to his little company that the president of the General Conference, Elder O. A. Olsen, would be on hand August 10, 1895, to dedicate the church. And on that date Elder Olsen consecrated the little church with a sermon on the worldwide outreach of the third angel's message.

After the dedicatory sermon, church treasurer Will Palmer itemized all building and church costs, including lumber, paint, seats, pulpit, and a little labor that had been hired. The bill: $160. Then Palmer calmly announced that the entire bill had been paid and that the church could claim $20 to its credit. After a short gasp, the little congregation responded with fervent hallelujahs. It was a happy surprise, since the members were expecting a long, hard, uphill pull.

At first they had planned to spend only $100 on the church. There would be no battens to cover the cracks between the upright planks of the walls, no paint outside, no ceiling, bare rafters above, and only thirty-five canvas camp stools plus a few additional planks to sit on.

But they knew that since the Lord had opened the way for the church to be started, He would not let the job go half done. The General Conference sent $25, the Battle Creek church $46. Dr. John Harvey Kellogg $10, Pacific Press workers $10, a layman in Ohio named Smouse $15, and George Lay $5. All these contributions, plus what was raised in Mississippi from the workers and members, had more than paid for the church.—**Ronald D. Graybill,** *Mission to Black America,* **1971, pp. 56, 58-60.**

2

Whipped and Shot for Their Faith

Well, the blow has fallen. A mob of the best planters along the Yazoo River called at the chapel at Calmar, and called Bro. [Dan] Stephenson[117] from his room, took him in buggy to Redwood, put him on the cars, and paid his fare to a station up the line. They were all kindness to him, but told him it was me[118] they were after. He is a Southern man, but I was the responsible one.

From the chapel they went to the house of Bro. [William H.] Casey,[119] but he had learned of the matter and got out of their way. Next they went to the house of Bro. [N. W.] Olvin,[120] who is impetuous and injudicious in his talk, and had said some things which maddened them. They took him out and whipped him. His wife, in trying to escape, was shot in the leg. I am told that I shall not be allowed [t]o operate along the Yazoo River between Yazoo City and Vicksburg. The difficulty arises from the assistance we have been giving to the colored people. This we find maddens the [white] people. The mob was made up of the best farmers, and not of the irresponsible class, and they are very determined.—**Portion of**

letter from James Edson White to his mother, Ellen G. White, written from Yazoo City, Mississippi, May 14, 1899.

Two weeks ago tonight a mob of about 25 white men came to our church at Calmer [sic.] at about midnight. They brought out brother [sic.] [Dan] Stephenson our worker, and then looted the church, burning book[s], maps, charts, etc. They hunted for Brother [William H.] Casey, our leading colored brother of that place, but he had escaped in time so they did not reach him. They then went to the house of Brother [N. W.] Olvin, called him out, and whipped him with a cow-hide. I think they would have killed him if had not been for a friendly white man who ordered them to stop whipping after they had struck a few blows. They did not pay any attention to him at first, but he drew his revolver, and said the next man who struck a blow would hear from him, and then they stopped. During the time they shot at Brother Olvin's wife, and struck her in the leg, but did not hurt her seriously. They took Brother Stephenson to the nearest railway station, put him on the cars, and sent him out of the country. They posted notice on the church forbidding me to return, and forbidding the steamer Morning Star to land between Yazoo City and Vicksburg.

The whole difficulty arose from our efforts to aid the colored people. We had given them clothing where in need, and food to those who were hungry, and had taught them some better ideas about farming, introduced different seeds such as peanuts, beans, etc., that bring a high price, etc., and this the whites would not stand.—**Portion of letter from James Edson White to his mother, Ellen G. White, written from Battle Creek, Michigan, May 25, 1899.**

We have had stirring times in our work in the South, and I inclose the copy I have written out to print so that I can send some around to friends that are interested in the work. I do not want it printed in any paper, for the quieter we keep in this matter the better it will be for the work in the south. O, Mother, we praise God that He in his infinite mercy gave us wisdom to so act in this matter that the camp of the enemy is alarmed as was often the case of the enemies of the people of God in olden times. I feel that it is a great evidence that God is with us in the work, that we are given wisdom to meet properly the difficulties brought upon us by the enemy. I tell you it was one of the trials of my life to give over every thought of retribution to those wicked people, but the Lord gave me the victory before I met the brother who was whipped,[121] and when I met him I suppose I had the greatest need of wisdom that I ever had. Poor, bruised, wounded, suffering man in both mind and body. It made my heart ache as I met him and saw the evidence of the awful ordeal through which he had passed. O, I praise God with all my heart that He gave me words for that poor, afflicted soul that drew him near to God and to us his staunch friends. And what a joy it was as the comforting words came to me as fast as I could use them, and how rejoiced I was when I saw that the Lord was working with him. And when he finally surrendered his own ideas of vengeance to the Lord, and became willing to let Him do the work of avenging his wrongs, how happy he became. Then he became as a little child. I then asked him, "What will you do with your Winchester rifle?" "Sell it" was his reply. But I knew he could not get for it what he paid, and also that he was not able to lose anything on it, and I was determined that the temptation should be removed. So I told him to take it back where it had been bought and get what he could for it, and I would make up whatever loss there was in the transaction. He asked Bro. Grimes to go and get it and sell it for him, and he would stay with us till it was done. He was stopping at the home of Bro. Grimes. So Bro. Grimes sold it back to the dealer from whom it was bought. The loss was $3.00, and I gave him the money. I have always been glad that I did it.——**Portion of letter from James Edson White to his mother, Ellen G. White, written from Battle Creek, Michigan, June 9, 1899.**

3

Trouble on the Yazoo River

[In the pamphlet <u>The Southern Work</u>, with the subtitle "(Mob Violence)," James Edson White described the predicament of the workers on the mission boat "Morning Star." The pamphlet, printed in Battle Creek, Michigan, is dated June 9, 1899.]

Many of our friends have been asking about reports that have been coming regarding mob violence at different points along the Yazoo River, where the Southern Missionary Society has been operating. To give any adequate statement of the situation requires considerable writing. Hence, to save time and yet give a more satisfactory idea of what has been done, the following printed statement has been prepared.

Toward the close of last December Elders [G. A.] Irwin and [I. H.] Evans were with us, looking over our work at different points. While with us, they made their home on the "Morning Star," and on it we traveled from place to place, inspecting the work from point to point, the trip ending at Vicksburg. The day after these brethren left us for Texas, word was received that an uprising against the Negroes was expected during the holidays, and further, that a body of masked men had gone to the river landing to destroy the "Morning Star;" but the boat was down the river, and so, by the good providence of God it escaped injury.

Not finding the boat, the mob searched for Brother [F. R.] Rogers,[122] our school teacher at Lintonia (a suburb of Yazoo City), but could not find him. But next day the ringleader called at the Lintonia chapel, where the school was held, and called Brother Rogers out, ordered him to stop the school, and leave town.

Just at this time all schools in the city were closed by the health officers on account of the breaking out of scarlet fever, which simplified matters for us considerably, and our school closed with the rest.

I immediately wired Brother Rogers to come to Vicksburg with his family, which he did. If an uprising were to occur, every effort would be made to throw the blame on us, and hence I preferred that all our company should be out of the city during the holiday season.[123]

But the better element of the city took the matter in hand, called a mass-meeting, at which the matter was denounced so vigorously that the disorderly element did not feel safe to engage in any lawless acts. But the fact that arms were sent to the place from Vicksburg and other points showed that a disturbance was contemplated, and bold statements had been made to that effect.

We had been warned that the "Morning Star" must stay away from Yazoo City, for it would not be allowed to land; but on the evening of Jan. 1, 1899, the steamer came to the city, and tied up at her usual mooring place.

All then gathered in the chapel of the "Star" and placed the boat and its people in the hands of our Lord for protection, asking that an angel guard and night-watch might be stationed on all decks of the boat. Later it was asked if we should put out a night-watch, but I could not feel it to be right to do this, after placing it all in the hands of One so much better able to protect us, and we all retired to rest as usual.

When the scarlet fever subsided, our school started again with the rest, and was very prosperous, the membership reaching about 200. From this time forward we had no trouble in our work, which was gaining strength and numbers rapidly, until May,[124] when we received a telegram from Brother [Dan] Stephenson, who was in charge of the work at Calmar, saying, "Do not go to Calmar until you hear from me." The next day a letter came stating that there had been mob violence at Calmar, the particulars of which are as follows:—

Thursday night, May 11, at 11 o'clock, a mob of about twenty-five white people and a few Negroes came to the chapel and called up Brother Stephenson, sending him away on the next train. They then looted the chapel, and burned the books, papers, charts, maps, etc., contained in it. A notice was then written and nailed up, forbidding us to return, or the "Morning Star" to land between Yazoo City and Vicksburg.

Then they went to the house of Brother [N. W.] Olvin, a colored man of considerable intelligence. He had given Bible readings in many places, and so was a marked man. They called him out, but he asked the privilege of reading a chapter and praying.

After this he went with the mob. His little daughter took him by the hand and went with him to the door, and as he left her, said, "Well, papa, I suppose you must give your life for the truth!" Before leaving the room a shot was fired by one of the mob, striking Sister Olvin below the knee, from which she is recovering very slowly.

Brother Olvin was taken out, stripped, and whipped with cowhide whips, three people taking part. But there was one whose heart had evidently been softened, for after a few blows had been struck, he told them to stop, for it was enough. But they did not stop, and he then drew a revolver and ordered them to stop, or he would shoot the next man who struck a blow. This had its effect, and Brother Olvin was released and allowed to go to his house.

Here he stayed until night after the Sabbath, but fearing further violence, he walked to Vicksburg that night. In response to a telegram I met him there the next Tuesday to plan for the future.

Brother Olvin is a strong-feeling, impulsive man, fearing nothing when aroused, and naturally vindictive. The ordeal through which he had passed had stirred these elements in his disposition to the very depths, and he was almost crazed. He had secured a Winchester through friends, and proposed to return and make reprisals. The man is known as an expert hunter and a dead shot; but when he accepted the truth he sold his rifle, for he felt he could no longer engage in such pursuits. But now he decided that he must not only avenge his own injuries, but that the work he proposed to do was also for the good of the cause.

In talking with him he would cling to the statement that he could pass by anything that had been done to him, but he could not get over the shooting of his wife. I assured him that this was always the case. We can endure every trial and every temptation, but just the one that comes to us. We fall under temptation, and excuse ourselves by saying the same thing: "We could have stood anything but this." Of course the devil knows our weak points, and that is just where he directs his strongest efforts.

Well, we talked Bible principles to him for over an hour. I quoted to him that "the wrath of man shall praise him, and the remainder shall he restrain." The thought was pressed upon him that God never allowed the wrath of man to break out against his people unless it was for the advancement of the work of God, or for the benefit of the individual. And God will restrain man whenever his wrath will not do this. This impressed him deeply.

Then came the text, "Vengeance is mine. I will repay, saith the Lord." I told him that if he would keep his hands out, God would take vengeance; and if he would only leave it in the hands of the Lord, he would be perfectly satisfied with the settlement that the Lord would make.

Then his attention was called to the fact that anything of this kind would arouse the whole white people in that part of the State, and would close it to our work, and probably shut out the work in the whole State, for we would be held responsible for the whole trouble.

The Lord worked on his heart, and at last he surrendered, and said he was willing to leave it all with the Lord. It was a pleasure to see the change that came over his countenance. Before he had a sullen, unhappy look. Poor man, he had passed through a terrible experience. It would shake many a man who has had better opportunities. But now his face had a look of relief. I asked him if he was not happier since he had decided to leave the matter with the Lord. He replied that he had not been so happy for five days.

Brother Olvin returned with me to the boat at Yazoo City to remain until some way should open for him.

A week later he went down the river on a steamer, stopping at the home of Brother Jones, four miles[125] from Calmar. From this point he made inquiries, and found that the white members of the mob were deciding that they had made a mistake; and the leader of the mob assured Brother Olvin that he could safely return to his home, and that he and others would see that he was protected. In fact, the leader of the mob is interesting himself to arrange so that meetings may be resumed in our little chapel.

I think they fear that some effort is under way to punish them for what they have done. I think they are troubled because we have been so quiet in this matter. They know they have put themselves where the strong hand of the law will punish them.—**James Edson White,** *The Southern Work (Mob Violence)*, **June 9, 1899, pp. 1-6**

4

Framed for Murder

The embattled Brother [N. W.] Olvin faced new trouble. A
Mr. H. B. Aden gave a Vicksburg paper certain distorted and
misleading details of a "murder." The newspaper printed the story
as fact. Edson questioned the reporter, who admitted that he had
only heard the story from some Negroes whom Edson immediately recognized as Brother Olvin's bitter enemies.

The persecution Brother Olvin had first felt when he became
an Adventist followed him to his new home, and this newspaper
headline was the result: "FIENDISH MURDER, Of a Little
Negro Boy by a Negro Man."

This story followed: "From Mr. H. B. Aden, who arrived in
this city on last night's 7 o'clock train, the following particulars of
some of the most brutal and horrible murders ever committed in
this section, are learned:

"Some months ago a Negro man giving the name of N. W.
Oliver [sic] came to the Valley Park section, and located on the

Dixie plantation where he taught school. A short time after his coming, he took up with a colored woman who had a child, a boy about five years old. Oliver took a dislike to the child, and on many occasions treated him shamefully.

"A few days ago, Oliver whipped the child most unmercifully, breaking the flesh in many places. The mother dared not utter a word of complaint, fearing the anger of the brute Oliver.

"After Oliver had beaten the child until but little life was left, he spread grease over its body and limbs in great profusion and then held it so near a hot stove that the flesh was blistered. The victim of this most unhuman [sic} treatment died while in the hands of Oliver.

"The latter was arrested, and committed without bail. If the full extent of his crime had been known before he was sent to jail, it is probable he would never have lived to have a trial.

"A gentleman from that section in the city today states that Oliver's life is in no wise secure even now."

Edson commented that "the spelling of the name of Olvin is about as true and accurate as the rest of the statement."

Edson's only hope of saving Brother Olvin was to set the record straight in the *Gospel Herald* and to raise money to defend him in court. Olvin never taught school. He simply cultivated a piece of land like all his neighbors. He did not "take up with a colored woman who had a child," but an orphan boy, wandering homeless, was taken in by his own family and treated as one of their own children.

The boy had previously been exposed to smallpox, and soon came down with the disease. And although Olvin was living in poverty, he nursed the boy back to health. The boy did need correcting, for he was caught stealing from the neighbors, but the charges of cruelty were completely false.

After he had been nursed through his attack of smallpox, the boy came down with dysentery. One day he was lying on the porch, five feet above the ground. Brother Olvin was in the house lying down, himself sick with a fever. The boy tried to get up, but was seized with an attack of dizziness, fell off the porch, hit his head on the rim of a washtub, and fractured his skull. He died that night.

The coroner's jury included some of the same enemies of Olvin who had invented the murder story.

It was months before Edson could post the $1,500 bail and release Olvin from Jail. The sick and frightened man stayed on board the *Morning Star* until his trial.

Edson advertised in the *Gospel Herald* to raise money for the "Olvin Defense Fund." But Olvin's enemies were taxed through their church to raise a fund to secure his conviction. Any member who would not pay was put out of the church. The difficulty in getting favorable witnesses from such a community is not hard to imagine.

Olvin's case finally came to trial. The spurious name given him in the newspaper dispatch seems to have stuck, and court records always refer to him as N. W. Oliver. His judge was named, ironically enough, Patrick Henry. Henry was a former United States Congressman from Mississippi and a member of the state constitutional convention which wrote the laws designed to keep Negroes from voting.

However, in Olvin's extreme circumstances, Judge Henry turned out to be his only chance for life. At first he pleaded "not guilty" to the charge of murder. Fifty names were drawn from which to select a jury.

The records indicate that Brother Olvin dropped his plea from "not guilty" to the murder charge. Perhaps realizing that with no one to witness in his favor, and with a jury stacked against him, he would certainly be convicted of the murder charge. The gallows were built right into the jail where he had been held. The sketchy evidence seems to suggest that he pleaded guilty to the lesser charge of manslaughter to escape death and was sentenced to ten years in the state penitentiary.

Penitentiary reports follow him through the first four years of his sentence, but no reports were filed with the state governor during the final years of his sentence. What eventually happened to him is not known. But the earnest black man paid a high price for his decision to accept the Bible Sabbath and for his hope in his Lord's return.—**Ronald D. Graybill, *Mission to Black America*, 1971, pp. 138-141.**

Section VI

EDUCATIONAL INSTITUTIONS

1

Avondale College

Our work began in Australia in 1885, when Pastors [Stephen N.] Haskell, [John O.] Corliss, and [M. C.] Israel, also Brethren Henry Scott and William Arnold, came to this field. Mrs. Daniells and I[126] arrived in New Zealand in November, 1885. Sister White, her son W. C. White, and a number of other workers came here in the latter part of 1891.

By that time we must have had nearly a thousand Sabbath-keepers in Australia and New Zealand. Among them was a large number of fine young people. They had a great desire to take part in the proclamation of our message. But they were without the education and training which they felt they needed, and we had no educational facilities here with which to help them. So great was their burden to obtain the needed preparation for service, that they began crossing the Pacific to attend our schools in America. By the time Sister White came, some twenty or thirty had left us for the schools in the States. That was a large undertaking for our people financially. It was estimated that by the time these young people had returned to Australia, their expenses would have amounted to six or eight thousand pounds sterling. But we felt we must continue that expensive programme, for we saw no possibility of establishing a school in this country in the very near future.

I was elected president of the Australian Conference on the first day of January, 1892, and before the year was half gone a message came from Sister White stating that the Lord would have us establish a school for the education of our Australasian youth. This message was most welcome, but at that time it gave us most serious perplexity, for it demanded great things from a constituency small in numbers and poor in this world's goods. After a great deal of study and counsel we decided to start an "Australasian Bible School" in the city of Melbourne. We rented two houses in St. George's Terrace, on St. Kilda Road. We then notified all our people regarding our plans for the school, and suggested that all who desired to avail themselves of its advantages should begin immediately to prepare for entrance.

The first term of this school was held in the year 1892. As I recall, there were between twenty-five and fifty students present. Their ages ranged from about fifteen to fifty years. Sister White was present at the opening service and gave us an inspiring address. After speaking to us in a very direct way regarding the occasion, she seemed to lose sight of her immediate surroundings and directed our attention to the great mission fields to the north and east and west of us—China, India, South America, and Africa. Some of these great fields we had not yet entered, while in some of them we were just making a beginning. She told us most clearly and forcibly that a great work would yet be carried on in *ALL* these fields. To our amazement she assured us that what had been developed in North America would be repeated in all those lands. She astonished us more than ever by saying that young people who received their training in the Australasian school would be sent as missionaries to the lands mentioned. Personally, I was overwhelmed by the great scope of activity and development revealed to us. . . . . My poor mind was too narrow and my vision too short to follow such a great sweep of advance. But I have lived to see those staggering predictions fulfilled in every detail. . . .

The school proved so helpful and satisfactory to the students during the first year, that they sent out encouraging reports to parents and friends, which led so many others to decide to attend the next year that we found it necessary to rent another house in St. George's Terrace. Thus we were making progress in our new undertaking. But all the time we were being counselled through the Spirit of Prophecy that this was not the kind of school that was to be permanently established in Australia. The permanent school was to be located in a rural district away from the cities. . . .

We reminded Sister White of what it would mean to a small constituency, few of whom owned their homes, to purchase high-priced land, erect necessary buildings, and establish and equip manual trades departments. We told her that the task seemed utterly impossible. But she seemed blind and deaf to our representations, and steadily pointed to the "blue-print" of the school that had been shown her.

This led to the appointment of a committee to make diligent search for a suitable location in the country away from the large cities. There was much searching and much disappointment. Good land was found in suitable places, but the cost was absolutely prohibitive to us. We had no land owners to make us good offers. No community in all the country had any interest in our proposal to establish a school on the land. Everywhere we faced cold, high prices.

In our searching, we ran across a block of 1,500 acres[127] at Cooranbong, New South Wales, being offered at a very low price— about fourteen shillings[128] per acre. The price was surely alluring to men in our financial situation. In other places we had visited, land was priced at £15[129] and more per acre. But when we saw the low-priced place, and inspected the soil, we met with considerable disappointment. Much of the block was poor, sandy, hungry land. However, some of it seemed fairly good. Some members of our committee favoured the purchase of this land, but other members did not believe that the soil was good enough for our needs. But with all of us the price had great influence. Still we were divided in our views.

In this state of uncertainty and perplexity we invited Sister White to visit the place. We took bedding and food with us for camping, and on arrival took possession of two or three fishermen's huts near the land. After spending quite a full day going over the place, examining the soil, tracing the creeks, and studying the best points for the location of our buildings, we returned to the huts for the night. We made fires, partook of some food, and then gathered in one of the huts for counsel.

There was much discussion and decided difference of views regarding the suitability of the place. To all that was said, Sister White listened with interest and in silence. Finally we requested her to tell us her impressions. Her reply was, "I think, brethren, that we would better kneel down and ask the Lord to give us light and understanding. I see no need of any more discussion. If this is the place we should select for our school, let us ask the Lord to give us evidence of some kind, that will give us assurance that this is the right location."

This suggestion appealed to all of us, and we knelt down and prayed most earnestly for divine guidance and for assurance. Sister White was led to pray most fervently. In her supplication the burden came upon her to pray for the healing of one of our members present who seemed to be going down rapidly with tuberculosis.

When we arose from prayer this brother[130] told us that while Sister White was praying, there passed through his body something like an electric wave, and he felt himself healed. That occurred in the year 1894—thirty-four years ago. That man is alive and well today. He has never had a trace of tuberculosis since that night of prayer in the fisherman's hut.

Sister White said, "Brethren, God is here with us. Why did He come so near and grant us this signal blessing? I accept it as evidence that we are in the right place." We all felt the same, and we agreed to take that property. We went on, made the contract for it, paid a deposit, and arranged for the transfer of the title.

But later some of us began to weaken and feel uneasy about the quality of the soil. In our perplexity it was proposed that we get the Government land expert in Sydney to examine the land and give us an expert analysis. The expert came out and gave the land a careful examination. When he had finished we took him to dinner without asking for an expression of his opinion. When dinner was over, we gathered on the verandah to hear what he had to say. His statement in brief was this: Gentlemen, I am sorry to have to tell you that this soil is worthless. It won't support a bandicoot (a large field rat). The wisest thing for you to do is to abandon all thought of making this place your school farm. To forfeit your deposit will be a small loss in comparison with what you will have if you locate on this block of land.

He returned to Sydney, wrote out a full analysis, placed one copy in the Government files and placed another copy in our hands.

It is needless to say that this report from a man who was supposed to know the value of soils in Australia, revived and increased our perplexity. After receiving this report the committee requested Brother [W. C.] White and me to lay it before Sister White. This was a painful and embarrassing task. When we had finished our statement, she calmly asked: Is there no God in Israel to inquire of, that ye have gone to the god of Ekron for counsel? Then she reminded us of that night of prayer and healing in the fisherman's hut. She told us that from that night she had felt no anxiety about the location, that her mind was at rest. But she said, "You may go on looking for a better place, and when you find one that satisfies you, I shall be glad to go with you to see it. But my spirit is at rest now." What could we say to this?

After reporting our interview to our brethren, we all decided to look no farther, but to go on with the place we had selected and hope for the best.—**Excerpt from part two of Elder A. G. Daniells' address, Monday night, June 25, 1928, at the**

New South Wales Ministerial Institute, printed in the
***Australasian Record*, August 20, 1928, pp. 1, 2.**

Our next problem was to pay for the land that we had secured at Cooranbong, for our school. We had no money. As president of the Conference, it fell to me to lead out in raising it. My courage was at a low ebb. I seemed unable to interest the brethren and persuade them to give toward the enterprise. But after months had passed with nothing done, I learned that Sister White had borrowed £1,000[131] and paid for the land. Somehow that made a powerful impression upon my heart. I felt condemned, and I knelt down and confessed my sin in allowing my unbelief and dallying course to increase the burden and perplexity and heart sorrow of the Lord's servant. From that day my faith, courage, and zeal in that school never wavered. I was able to throw all my energies into the enterprise.

The problem of erecting buildings and providing the furniture and equipment required for the sort of school we were undertaking to establish, was very great for the small number of members we had in Australasia. We were obliged to begin in a very small and inexpensive way.

Our first unit consisted of a small dormitory and a dining hall and kitchen. We were so short of funds that in finishing the dormitory we were obliged to call for volunteers to give free labour. Among others who responded were Pastor [Stephen] Haskell and his wife [Hetty]. At the night work one would hold a lighted candle while the other drove the nails. Only those who were on the ground and passed through the struggle can realise how great it was.

When those two buildings were finished and furnished, the first term of what was to be known as the Australasian Missionary College was begun. The first day of our new school (April 28, 1897) led us to realise that we were not to "despise the day of small things," for we opened the term with four teachers and ten students. Because of the long delay, the perplexities and the discouragements in getting the location and providing the buildings and equipment, our people had nearly lost heart. But when it was known that the school had really opened, a new interest was awakened, and before the term closed there were fifty or sixty students in attendance.

Thus far we had endeavoured to pull through without calling upon the General Conference for assistance, but we found the grade so steep and so long that we finally appealed to the brethren in America for help. They promptly responded by offering to appropriate a sum equal to the amount we would raise within a reasonable limit. This gave us great encouragement, and with good heart our people in Australasia undertook to raise their share.

In the meantime we went on with our building operations, paying our sharing and running in debt for theirs, expecting that when they heard what we had raised, they would promptly send their share. We gave our carpenters and plasterers, and the business men from whom we purchased material, assurance that we would be receiving money from American to meet our obligations. We fully expected to receive this money by a certain mail from America. But we were doomed to a terrible disappointment. Instead of receiving a draft, we were notified that owing to financial depression, they were unable to send their part, and advised us to delay building operations until the financial situation had improved in America. But we had already gone on with our building, and we had no money to meet our obligations.

This disappointment was terrible. We knew not what to do. The members of the School Board were depressed. Naturally we blamed ourselves for going ahead [and building] without the money. After a long, fruitless discussion we adjourned in discouragement until the next morning. I went to my room, but I could not sleep. I rolled and tossed and perspired. I was in agony of mind. I rose and went out in the bush where I could be alone. I had to have help from some source. It seemed to me that my nerves would go to pieces. I had to have help to find a way out of this situation we were in.

There in the dark I prayed and cried to God to send us help. I prayed on and on until the morning light began to appear. With all my heart, I cried to the Lord to send me an answer; to give me some light. And there came to me a most positive answer: "I have delivered thee. I will meet this situation. Be of good cheer." The presence of God as so powerful that I could not stay on my knees, I could only lie on the ground and thank and praise God for deliverance. Something was going to be done by the Almighty, and I knew it as well as I knew that I lived.

I went back to my room, washed, and went down to the committee room. The brethren were there looking very sombre and heavy. I went in smiling and said, Brethren, be of good cheer. We are delivered. Our obligations are met.

They could not understand what I meant, and I could not tell all. But I told them that if they would allow me to go to Sydney and Melbourne and Adelaide, I was sure that in about two weeks I could send them every pound required to meet our obligations. They consented, and I was on the train at eight o'clock that morning.

And at once God began to do wonderful things for our deliverance. While I was on the train that day, a cable came from a brother in New Zealand, addressed to me, asking if I could make use of five hundred pounds.[132] . . . I had not asked him for the money. Why did he do this? I know why. The Lord moved him to do it. He sent the money at once.

On my arrival in Melbourne, I was thrown into a new perplexity. I met one of our sisters there from whom we [earlier] had borrowed £300[133] to use in our building operations. This money was due in three days. I did not want to fail to meet this payment. I endeavoured to get her to renew the loan for another year. But she declined with a firm statement that she would expect payment day after tomorrow.

I was being entertained by Brother W. D. Salisbury. I went to my bed that night greatly troubled. The next morning while I was praying, and reminding the Lord of His promise that He had delivered us, there came to me a very clear impression to get an answer from the Bible. Then I did what I had never done before, and I do not know that I have ever done it since. I put my finger on the margin and opened the Book. The very first words I read were these:

"Thy God whom thou servest continually, He will deliver thee." Dan. 6:16. I wrote in the margin of my Bible, "Salisbury's room, 7:20 a.m., 5/4/99."[134] That evening at five o'clock, I wrote, "Fulfilled 5 p.m., 5/4/99." I seldom tell the marvellous [sic.] way in which it was fulfilled, but I shall do so on this occasion.

I went to the Echo Office [our publishing house] that morning and waited to see what would occur. After the noon hour, I called Brethren [N. D.] Faulkhead and Salisbury together and told them that three hundred pounds must be delivered to that sister the next day. Brother Faulkhead told us of a man who had recently offered to lend the Echo Office a large sum of money. We went at once to see this man. But he had disposed of the money in another way.

Brother Faulkhead next suggested that we might be able to get it from our Echo Office bank. But it was then 4 p.m. and the bank was closed. He suggested that we should go to the banker's home and see him privately. I confess that that looked very uncertain to me. But we decided to make the effort. The bank was on a corner, and we had to pass the door on the way to the banker's house. As we were hurrying past the door of the bank, we saw that it was open about the width of a man. Brother Faulkhead rushed in and I after him as fast as we could move. We found the banker and his assistant with the contents of the vault spread out on the counters. They were getting affairs in shape for the visit of a London bank inspector.[135] The banker looked up at us in amazement and said, "Faulkhead, how did you get into this bank?"

"We walked in." was the reply.

"Yes, I know, but how did you get the door open?" said the banker, "for I shut, bolted, locked, and chained that door myself. How did you get it open?"

"We did not touch it, it was open," was all we could say.

Well, brethren, we knew right then that an angel opened that door. The banker was so shocked that he looked pale. When he could compose himself, he asked what we wanted. Brother Faulkhead said, "We want to see you in your private office." As soon as we were seated, we told him that we wanted three hundred pounds to meet an obligation the next morning. "What security can you give?" "Only our word tonight, but we will give something more later."

Then and there that banker counted out three hundred shining [gold] sovereigns and placed them in our hands. The next morning I went to our sister with this money and met our obligation.

These experiences, I can assure you, made a deep impression on my mind—that assurance under the tree at Cooranbong, the assurance in Brother Salisbury's room that morning, the open door of the bank, and the money in my hands that evening, and that is why I wrote "Fulfilled" in the margin of my Bible.

On Sabbath, two days later, I went over to the Prahan church to preach. I was so overcome, and so moved by my experiences I was passing through, that I could scarcely control my feelings. The audience was greatly moved. The sister to whom I had paid the £300 was present. I saw that she was greatly moved. When the meeting was out, she came up to me and said, "Brother Daniells, will you meet me in the bank Monday morning at nine o'clock?" When I met her she said, "I have not had a minute's peace since I took that money from you. I will give it back to you, and I will give you £75[136] extra as penalty for taking it." I accepted it, and she never, I understand, withdrew it from the school.

Then I went to Adelaide, and while looking for help, I had an impression that I ought to go to a certain family for money. This sister's husband was not a member of the church, consequently I felt reluctant about asking for his money. I kept trying to tell them what I was after, but I seemed unable to do so. Finally, the sister said, "Brother Daniells, I think my husband ought to make our cause his banker, don't you?" That was the help I needed, and I placed before them what I had come to see them about. The result was that this man placed in my hands £400[137] as a loan.

Next I went to see a brother while he was working at his carpenter's bench. I ventured to ask for one hundred pounds.[138] He said, "Come around at two o'clock and I will have it ready for you." When I called he said, "I have been thinking about this and feel that you can do with another hundred." I surely could. "Well," he said, "let me think about it until tomorrow morning." I went over to see him the next morning and he said, "I had decided to let you have the two hundred pounds,[139] but I do not feel quite satisfied. I think I will make it three hundred pounds."[140]

Thus the money came in from all quarters, and in two weeks from the night the Lord gave me the assurance that He had delivered us, I had sent the school enough money to pay all our bills. **—Excerpt from part three of Elder A. G. Daniells' address, Monday night, June 25, 1928, at the New South Wales Ministerial Institute, printed in the *Australasian Record*, August 27, 1928, pp. 1, 2.**

2

Oakwood College

I . . . heard that Sister White had said there ought to be a school located in the country near Nashville, Tennessee, or in northern Alabama, since the racial feelings were not so bad there as in other places in the South. A committee had been to Nashville and some other places but could not find any location that appealed to them. They were on their way to northern Alabama to see what they could find. Early the next morning before starting they gathered in the living room for prayer. It was the custom of Brother and Sister Chambers to pray three times a day, morning, noon, and night. I was deeply impressed by the earnestness of the prayers of these men as they asked the Lord to help them find the place He had in mind for a colored school. They were so earnest that they shed tears over it. After prayer they went to the railway station, took the train to Huntsville, and were directed out to a farm which was for sale. They said after they entered the grounds that they had a feeling that this was the place the Lord had in mind for the school.

After careful investigation, they put down a deposit to hold the farm until they could report their findings to Battle Creek, Michigan.

I was at Battle Creek attending the Industrial Preparatory School when a special offering was planned for the colored work to raise a fund to help buy that farm on which the General Conference wished to establish a school. Everyone was asked to give a dollar. Many did not have the dollar to give, and they sacrificed a meal a day, thereby saving the money for an offering on the following Sabbath to help the colored work.

In due time the money was raised and the purchase was made. —Knight, *Mississippi Girl*, pp. 208, 209.

3

Atlantic Union College

"*Whereas,* A school has been opened in South Lancaster among S. D. Adventists; and—

"*Whereas,* It has required sacrifice on the part of its founders to start the enterprise, and will require still more to carry it on successfully; therefore— . . .

"*Resolved,* That we, the young ladies of the South Lancaster school, feeling anxious to do our part in sustaining the same, will be responsible for the laundry work, and for all necessary repairs in the clothing of the young men who donate their time in cultivating land for the benefit of the school; and that we will be glad to help in any other way whenever opportunities present themselves."—**Ella Robinson,** *Man of Action,* **p. 52.**

Section VII

HEALTH INSTITUTIONS

1

Battle Creek Sanitarium

The name "The Western Health Reform Institute" was chosen for the new health institution that had been called for in the view given to Mrs. White at Rochester, New York,[141] and related by her before the General Conference assembly.[142] Of the initial steps taken to launch this new enterprise, Elder J. N. Loughborough later wrote:

"The question arose, 'How can we, in our condition of limited means, obtain and control a health institution?" Brother James White was at that time in a critical condition of health and could not take upon himself the management of the enterprise; so the matter seemed to fall upon the Michigan Conference Committee, of which I[143] was at that time president. The committee, with a few of the leading members in Battle Creek, counseled and prayed over the matter and said, 'We will pledge to the enterprise, venturing out on what is said in the testimony, though it looks to us like a heavy load for us to hold up.'"—**"Sketches of the Past,"** No. 133, in *Pacific Union Recorder*, January 2, 1913.

Drawing up a subscription paper, Elder Loughborough went first to J. P. Kellogg,[144] reminding him of the testimony given by Mrs. White and of the decision to establish a health institution. Taking the paper, Brother Kellogg wrote his name in a bold hand, and opposite the figures $500. He assured Elder Loughborough that he would venture this much in the enterprise whether it should succeed or not. "Understand," he said, "that five hundred collars is a seed to start the institution, sink or swim."—*Medical Missionary*, May, 1899, Extra.

With this encouraging beginning, a meeting was called of the members of the church in Battle Creek, and opportunity was given to others to subscribe to the enterprise. Another $500 was pledged by Mrs. E. G. White, and $250 by J. M. Aldrich. Two other pledges for $100, two for $50, and eleven for $25 each brought a total of $1,825 raised at denominational headquarters.

Elder J. N. Andrews brought the matter before a monthly meeting of the church in Olcott, New York, and the members there pledged $800. Thus, with a start of $2,625 raised in the two churches, the campaign was launched. Circulars were prepared for mailing to each church and to prospective investors, soliciting the purchase of dividend-bearing shares of $25. Each church was requested to call a meeting at which the matter should be presented, with solicitation for cash and pledges. The subscription list was opened in the *Review and Herald* for June 19, 1866 . . . and the progress of the fund was reported weekly.—**Dores E. Robinson,** *The Story of Our Health Message*, 1965, pp. 149-151.

At the time appointed the institution was opened for the reception of patients. Dr. [H. S.] Lay[145] and Dr. Phoebe Lamson[146] constituted the medical staff. So with "two doctors, two bath attendants, one nurse (untrained), three or four helpers, one patient, any amount of inconveniences, and a great deal of faith in the future of the institution and the principles on which it was founded" (*Medical Missionary*, January, 1894) was begun an institution destined to become world famous, and whose cumulative influence cannot be estimated.—**ibid., p. 153.**

2

Loma Linda University

Purchase of Paradise Valley and Glendale Sanitariums

By the turn of the century, Seventh-day Adventists had established twenty-six sanitariums and treatment rooms in the United States and abroad. Under added appeals by Mrs. White, in 1904 and 1905 they established three more sanitariums in Southern California: in Glendale, Paradise Valley, and Loma Linda.

From her home near St. Helena, California, Ellen White had predicted in 1902 that "unoccupied properties" would soon become available in Southern California; properties that could be purchased "far below the original cost" and used as sanitariums.[147] She assured church leaders that "unusual bargains" might be found. "For months," she wrote, "the Lord has given me instruction that He is preparing the way for our people to obtain possession, at little cost, of properties on which there are buildings that can be utilized in our work."[148]

The Paradise Valley facility (now the Paradise Valley Hospital) represented an investment of $25,000. It was offered to the Seventh-day Adventist church for $12,000. In 1904 it was purchased for $4,000—"far below the original cost," just as Ellen White had predicted. The Glendale Hotel (now the Glendale Adventist Medical Center) represented an investment of $50,000. It was offered to Seventh-day Adventists for $26,000. In 1904 it was purchased for only $12,000—"far below the original cost."

Purchase of the Loma Linda Sanitarium

Though to all appearances it seemed financially impossible, even foolhardy, Ellen White had been instructed in vision that the church should acquire not only these two properties but also a third, and that all three should become sanitariums which would be centers of medical and spiritual healing.

That same year Ellen White instructed John Burden, manager of the St. Helena Sanitarium (now St. Helena Hospital and Health Center) near San Francisco, to look between Riverside, San Bernardino, and Redlands for this third property which she had seen in vision. In March 1904, Burden found seventy-six acres[149] of property four miles[150] from Redlands which matched her description, and inquired about the price. He learned that the facilities on the property had been built in the 1880s by land speculators, or "boomers," as those who built boom towns in the West were called. The speculators had named the proposed resort community Mound City. But they went bankrupt, then sold out to a group of eighty physicians and forty businessmen from Los Angeles who wanted to develop Mound City into a health resort. The new owners renamed the property "Loma Linda" ("Hill Beautiful"), and invested over $155,000 in new buildings, redecorating, furnishings, and other improvements. But their effort failed and the stockholders were desperate.

For months Loma Linda was deserted except for a caretaker and grazing sheep. People in the surrounding community nicknamed the hill "Lonesome Linda." Burden was told that the $155,000 property could be purchased for $110,000. But $110,000 was out of the question. He left.

Mrs. White urged him to return. This time the price was lowered to $85,000. Still, $85,000 might as well have been $85,000,000. The fourteen hundred church members in Southern California were already supporting a large building program of new churches and health institutions. And church headquarters—the General Conference of Seventh-day Adventists in Washington, D.C.—had just established a "no-debt policy" and could not help finance any new institutions. Again Burden left and told Mrs. White the new price.

An important educational center

[Ellen] White said that someday thousands of people would be moving into the area and Loma Linda would become not only a center of medical and spiritual healing but also "an important educational center" to prepare medical missionaries. How were these ideals to be realized? In 1905 Ellen White's 541-page book, *Ministry of Healing*, was published. It revealed Christ as the true Gospel Medical Missionary and outlined how to follow in His footsteps: A school should be built to provide practical experience in Gospel medical missionary work. Mrs. White urged Burden to return to Loma Linda a third time. This time Burden asked whether the owners were really serious about selling Loma Linda and what would be the bottom dollar they would accept. They said they would settle for $40,000. Although the sum still seemed astronomical, Burden inspected the property more closely. He found that it included thirty-one acres[151] of grain land; twenty-two acres[152] of alfalfa, vegetable gardens, an apricot orchard and a barn; and a twenty-three acre terraced hill covered with orchards, gardens, beautifully landscaped lawns, scores of tall shade trees and pepper trees filled with canaries, a profusion of flowers and ornamental shrubs, carriage drives, and over a mile[153] of gracefully curving concrete walks. On the summit of the hill were several cottages, a large recreation hall, and a four-story, sixty-four-room frame hotel. The buildings, in excellent condition, were lighted with electricity and heated with steam. Water was piped through the premises from a large artesian well. The property also included $12,000 to $15,000 worth of equipment and supplies that had never been used. Burden decided to purchase the land and buildings.

Terms of the purchase

The terms were $5,000 down and, within the next few months, three monthly payments of $5,000 each—the first half of the purchase price. The remaining $20,000 was to be paid at the end of three years. On Friday afternoon, May 26, 1905, lawyers came to sign the contract of sale. Because it was nearing sunset that Friday evening and "the Sabbath" was about to begin, Burden and the few church members with him decided to postpone the signing of the papers until Monday.

On Sunday, May 28, Burden received a telegram from G. W. Reaser, president of the Southern California Conference, who at the time was in Washington, D.C. It said, "Developments here warrant advising do not make deposit on sanitarium." It is not difficult to understand the directive since it seemed certain that there would be no funds available to make either the deposit or the payments. But, at Mrs. White's urging, and with her assurance that the Lord would provide, on Monday Burden paid $1,000 borrowed on his personal note to secure an option to buy Loma Linda.[154] This $1,000 was to be forfeited if the down payment or monthly payments could not be made.

Two weeks later, on Monday morning, June 12, 1905, Mrs. White came to Loma Linda for the first time. As she was taken on an inspection tour she said repeatedly that she recognized it as the very place she had seen in vision nearly two years before (in the fall of 1903 and also on October 10, 1901). She sat down in the parlor and spoke of the educational work that was to be carried forward in Loma Linda.

Encouraged by Burden's example, local Adventists contributed another $4,000 to complete the June 15 down payment, though none had any idea how they would meet the July payment—another $5,000—due in one month. On June 20, delegates of nearly all the twenty-two churches in the Southern California Conference met to consider purchasing the Loma Linda property. The conference president told the delegates of the importance of the decision they would make that day. According to the minutes of the meeting, "He then stated that Sister White had said that this sanitarium should be the principal training school on this coast. At this point Sister White interrupted him and said, 'This will be.'"[155] Finally, the Southern California Conference Committee agreed to support the project.—**Richard A. Schaefer, Legacy, Daring to Care, 1995, pp. 157-160.**

[Elder John Burden later described the spirit of sacrifice that characterized some of the supporters of Loma Linda, as well as the miraculous timing of a key payment.]

The [Southern] Conference Committee[156] at the first meeting, in the Los Angeles church,[157] had taken the ground that they would not assume the obligation unless the delegates representing all the churches should authorize it. But before this final meeting of all the delegates could be called to decide the matter, another $4,000 must be raised and paid in to the agent to complete the first payment,[158] or we should fail in carrying out our part of the contract and might lose the $1,000 already paid in, and the deal would be repudiated.

For the Conference to have furnished the funds for a portion of the payment would have signified that they had accepted responsibility for all the payments. The uncertainty that the Conference would later accept the responsibility had weakened the confidence of some with means who would otherwise have helped. However, we decided to do our best to secure the necessary money to meet the payment that was due.

We first asked a Sister Bell Baker, now sleeping, how she felt regarding the securing of Loma Linda.

"I do not see why any one should hesitate," she replied. "It seems plain that we should have it."

We said, "Are you willing to risk a thousand dollars in it?"

"Yes," she replied.

"You may lose it," we reminded her.

"Well," she said, "I will risk it," and she gave us a thousand dollars as a loan.

We next made the same suggestion to a Brother, and he responded with $2,000. We conferred with Elder R. S. Owen, who had made the suggestion as to where we might find the previous thousand dollars for the first payment. He was unable to make any recommendation as to who might help us, but he said: "I have not the money, but here is my property; you may put a mortgage on it for a thousand dollars, to secure the money."

We found that it was not necessary to put a mortgage on the property, as his word was good for the amount, so we put in the second $1,000 of the $2400 we received. On the very day it was due we were enabled to meet the second payment [of the first $5,000 due] on the property, which insured holding it until the delegates from the churches should decide what responsibility, if any, the Conference should assume.

The decision to purchase

Just about this time Elder G. A. Irwin, Vice-president of the General Conference, passed through Southern California on his way to attend a general meeting of the Pacific Press Publishing Company, at Mountain View. We felt that his presence was timely, and, after relating to him the situation regarding the purchase of Loma Linda, earnestly requested that he attend the coming meeting in Los Angeles. It was arranged that he should return in time to reach Los Angeles on the 19th of June, the day before the meeting appointed, to make the final decision regarding the attitude of the Southern California Conference toward the Loma Linda enterprise.

We met the train on his arrival at Los Angeles, and accompanied him to Loma Linda, that he might see the place for himself. We spent the night there and returned the following morning. From the Los Angeles station we hurried to the church and found the meeting in progress. The church was crowded with delegates, but seats were found for us on the rostrum.

Mrs. White was already speaking. In her talk she set forth the high and exalted character of the work that should be done in Medical Missionary work in the Southern California field. Once more she related the descriptions that had been given her in vision, of properties that should be secured and utilized for sanitarium work, and expressed herself clearly as being in favor of securing the Loma Linda property.

The President of the Southern California Conference[159] had felt that before acting on the question of the securing of Loma Linda, the delegates should have a clear understanding of the financial obligations already resting upon the Conference, that they might better realize what would be involved in this added responsibility. For this reason he had prepared papers ready to be distributed, giving the figures in question. At the close of Mrs. White's talk he took the floor, and was beginning to speak of the very real difficulties, when Elder Irwin arose, and the speaker courteously granted him the privilege of speaking.

"I confess that this is a gigantic undertaking that you are facing," he began. Without minimizing the difficulties, he encouraged the hearers to believe that when God made a call through His servant He would open the seas of difficulty before them as they advanced by faith. He briefly rehearsed the experiences of the denomination as they had followed the counsels that had come through the Spirit of Prophecy in opening up new fields and establishing institutions. Owing to his long experience in the ministry, during several years of which he had been President of the General Conference, he was able to speak from personal observance and contact with the problems of the denomination and of Mrs. White's relation to them. He could testify of the signal blessing of God that had rested upon the enterprises and upon the workers as they had responded to the messages calling for forward moves. . . .

While appreciating the tremendous difficulties facing the brethren of the Southern California Conference as they faced the proposition of purchasing and developing Loma Linda, yet seeing Sister White had spoken so clearly regarding it, with his knowledge of past experiences he could only counsel them to face the situation courageously and to move forward in faith.

When Elder Irwin finished his appeal a lady arose in the audience, a daughter of General Otis, of the Los Angeles Times [sic.]. She had recently accepted the faith of Seventh-day Adventists.

"I cannot understand," she said, "why any one should hesitate. It seems to me as clear as day that we should have Loma Linda. I have ten thousand dollars invested in worldly enterprises, and if the Lord will help me to release it I will gladly put it into Loma Linda. I have been praying that He would make me a pioneer in some enterprise."

While, as later developed, she was unable to secure the release of her money, as she desired, nevertheless her consecration was used of the Lord to help to turn the tide of public sentiment in favor of securing Loma Linda. Others followed her in the congregation, pledging their support to the move. When the resolution, formerly presented to the smaller gathering in the Los Angeles church, was read, it was carried by an overwhelming vote of the delegates of the twenty-two churches represented in the general meeting.

Securing the second payment

The time was drawing near when a second payment[160] of $5,000 must be paid on the purchase price of Loma Linda. We had approached every one whom we knew in Southern California who would be likely to help, and had written many letters, and had received returns of some. The Conference Committee were beginning to fear that the Conference credit would be jeopardized by this new undertaking, and urged that we try to get free from the financial responsibility by losing the $5,00 [$5,000] we had paid down. In our distress we mentioned that we believed we might secure money in the Sacramento and the San Joaquin churches, as we had often raised money there for the St. Helena Sanitarium, so the committee suggested that we ask the California Conference to permit us to solicit means among the church members in the Sacramento and San Joaquin valleys.

In harmony with this suggestion, we visited the California Conference[161] Committee and told them of our perplexities and needs. They reminded us that the Pacific Union Conference had advised the Southern California brethren not to invest in more sanitariums, and reminded us that we had gone contrary to this counsel. Because of this, and because of their own financial needs, they objected to granting us the privilege of soliciting in the territory of the California Conference. We returned home wondering where the needed money would come from.

As the day when the payment was due drew nearer, and no money was in sight, deep anxiety was felt by those carrying the financial responsibilities of the Conference. At last the day arrived, and the forenoon found the members of the Conference Committee in session in Los Angeles in deep perplexity. It seemed to some that we were unable to meet the payment and that the only way out of the difficulty was to acknowledge our inability to the agent of the property, and if we could not secure an extension of time we must forfeit the contract and lose the five thousand dollars already paid in.

But it was natural that some members of the committee who had from the first felt that it was unwise to accept the great responsibility, should seem to feel that circumstances had only proved the wisdom of their misgivings. In the face of the humiliating necessity, as it seemed, of losing the property, it was easy and natural to blame and censure those who had apparently pressed the matter through against sound reason and judgment.

Nevertheless, some remembered the clear words that had come through the Testimonies, and refused to give room to doubt, or to concede that there should be failure. Yet we knew not how relief would come. We suggested that the morning mail might bring relief. Soon after this the postman's steps were heard coming up the stairs. He opened the door and handed the mail to the one sitting nearest. Among the letters was one bearing the postmark "Atlantic City, N. J." We opened the letter and took out a draft for $5,000, just the amount needed for the payment.

We had previously received a letter from Mrs. White, dated July 10, 1905, in which she had said: "I want you to keep me posted about the money coming in with which to make the payments on the 'Loma Linda' property. I am writing the different ones, asking them to help at this time, and I think that we shall obtain means to make every payment."—Letter 197, 1905.

Probably one of those to whom Mrs. White had written, asking for money, was this sister at Atlantic City, N. J. The Lord had put it into her heart to respond and to mail the letter just at the time when our faith had been tested almost to the limit, that it might be revived and strengthened.

Needless to say, the feelings of those who had been critical were quickly changed. Eyes filled with tears, and the one who had been the most critical was the first to break the silence. With trembling voice, he said: "It seems that the Lord is in this matter." "Surely He is," was the reply, "and He will carry it through to victory." The influence that filled the room that day hushed the spirit of criticism. It was as solemn as the Judgment Day.

Soon we were at the bank window and had paid in the $5,000. As the receipt was taken from the counter a voice seemed to say, "See how nearly you missed that payment. How are you going to meet the next one within a month? In heart we answered, "It will surely come, even though we do not know the source," and our faith did not waver when the difficulties increased as we moved forward. We thanked God and took new courage in believing that the Lord was going before us.—**John A. Burden,** *The Divine Leadership Through the Spirit of Prophecy*, **unpublished manuscript, date unknown, White Estate Document File, No. 8a, pp. 85-88.**

Unlooked-for-funds from various persons enabled them to pay for the property in less than six months, thus gaining an additional discount of $1,100. The final purchase price was $38,900—"far below the original cost." The three properties, originally worth a total of $225,000, were purchased for $56,000—less than one-fourth of their original cost. In 1994 these three hospitals scheduled 56,644 patient-admissions.

In November of 1905, the Loma Linda Sanitarium and School of Nursing opened. During the first few weeks, the thirty-five Sanitarium employees, including physicians and nurses, learned that patient revenue ($16 to $25 per week per patient—which included medical care, meals, treatments twice a day, and a room) was not sufficient to meet the payroll. With strong faith to offset their deepening poverty, they cheerfully offered to work for room and board until the patronage increased. That winter there were only forty patients. But by June 30, 1906, Sanitarium accounts were over $1,000 in the black.—**Schaefer, *Legacy*, pp. 160, 161.**

Section VIII

PROBLEMS WITH SABBATH OBSERVANCE

1

Tennessee Chain Gangs

[In 1892, the National Religious Liberty Association, forerunner of the current Religious Liberty Department at the General Conference, issued a 12-page pamphlet entitled, <u>In the Chain-Gang for Conscience' Sake.</u> *It recounted the story of three Seventh-day Adventists who were forced to work in a chain gang in Tennessee for working on Sunday.]*

July 18, in the year of our Lord 1892, witnessed a sight that revives the memories of the religious persecutions of the Dark Ages. At Paris, Tenn., four Christian men had been lying in jail since June 3, 1892, for the crime (?) of following their "common avocations on Sunday, by working on the farm, plowing, hoeing," etc. The term of one having expired, the other three, after having lain in jail forty-four days, were, Monday, July 18, marched through the streets in company with some colored criminals, and put to work shoveling on the common highway. All three were men of families, one fifty-five and another sixty-two years of age.

As to the character of these men who were thus imprisoned and driven through the county seat of their county in the chain-gang, let the prosecuting attorney in the case, Mr. A. W. Lewis,[162] answer. In his argument before the court, May 27, referring to their prosecution, he made the following statement, as appears from a stenographic report of the trial:—

"It is regretted, because of the fact that otherwise [aside from their observing the seventh day as the Sabbath, and working on their farms on Sunday][163] they are good citizens."

These "good citizens" have suffered imprisonment and convict servitude, notwithstanding the constitution of Tennessee declares that "all men have a natural and indefeasible right to worship Almighty God according to the dictates of their own conscience; . . . that no human authority can, in any case whatever, control or interfere with the rights of conscience; and that no preference shall ever be given by law to any religious establishment or mode of worship."—*Art. 1, Sec. 3.*

In contradiction to this strong and explicit declaration of man's natural right to worship his God unmolested, the State of Tennessee has enacted the following law, which was handed down to

her from the theocracy of England through the State-Church period of North Carolina:—"Sec. 2289. If any merchant, artificer, tradesman, farmer, or other person, shall be guilty of doing or exercising any of the common avocations of life, or of causing or permitting the same to be done by his children or servants, acts of real necessity or charity excepted, on Sunday, he shall, on due conviction thereof before any Justice of the Peace of the county, forfeit and pay three dollars, one half to the person who shall sue for the same, the other half for the use of the county."

Tennessee has another statue providing for a penalty of not more than $100 for maintaining a nuisance, and the courts of Tennessee have decided that "a succession of such acts [Sunday work][164] becomes a nuisance and is indictable."

With this for a basis, the Grand Jury of Henry county found indictments against five members of the Seventh-day Adventist church who live on small farms near Springville, Tenn. The cases were tried at Paris, Tenn., May 27, 1892, before Judge W. H.

Swiggart. The defendants did not choose to employ counsel, but appeared in their own behalf.

Six witnesses were introduced by the prosecution, each of whom testified that he was not disturbed by the labor of the defendants on Sunday, and did not give the name of any person who was disturbed. The testimony introduced proved that W. S. Lowry had been seen at one time cutting fire-wood, and at another, loading wood on a wagon on Sunday; that J. Moon had been seen on one occasion cutting sprouts from his field on Sunday; that J. H. Dortch had been seen, on one Sunday only, plowing strawberries; and that James Stemm had followed his ordinary and common vocations on Sunday, no definite work on any definite Sunday being proved against him. Besides, in several instances their fields were not along any public road, and consequently a man could not be seen working in them, as the evidence proved, unless some one "chanced to pass that way."

Each one of the accused, when brought to trial, made a short statement of his position, and submitted his case to the jury. As an illustration of the defense of the accused, the statement of W. S. Lowry, whose case was heard first, is here appended:—

"I would like to say to the jury, that, as has been stated, I am a Seventh-day Adventist. I observe the seventh day of the week as the Sabbath. I read my Bible, and my convictions on the Bible are that the seventh day of the week is the Sabbath, which comes on Saturday. I observe that day the best I know how. Then I claim the God-given right to six days of labor. I have a wife and four children, and it takes my labor six days to make a living. I go about my work quietly, do not make any unnecessary noise, but do my work as quietly as possible. It has been proved by the testimony of Mr. Fitch and Mr. Cox, who live around me, that they were not disturbed. Here I am before the court to answer for this right that I claim as a Christian. I am a law-abiding citizen, believing that we should obey the laws of the State; but whenever they conflict with my religious convictions and the Bible, I stand and choose to serve the law of my God rather than the laws of the State. I do not desire to cast any reflections upon the State, nor the officers and authorities executing the law. I leave the case with you."

As evidence that these prosecutions are in the nature of religious persecution, that they are attempts to compel obedience to church dogmas, protected and promulgated by the statues and court decisions of the State of Tennessee, extracts from the plea of the State's Attorney J. W. Lewis,[165] before the jury, are herewith submitted:—

"While the Constitution guarantees to him the right to keep Saturday, and protects him in his worship while engaged in that worship; and if in his church others should disturb him, he would have the same safeguards thrown around him, and the same solemn protection given him in that worship that you have in your own church, yet *he must bow to the laws of the State of Tennessee; he must bow to the laws of this country; he must bow to the laws that have been made and recognized and must be enforced by the courts of this country*. And if he feels that it is his duty to keep Saturday, his Honor will charge that *the law makes him desist from his secular work on Sunday*. It is not a question of fact at all; it is only a question of law; because he does not dispute that he follows his everyday avocations, but admits it; he does not dispute that he follows the work on Sunday that he follows during the week, but admits it, and *gives as an excuse* that it is a conviction of his church belief."

"The people of Tennessee, by the laws, designate and point out a certain day as the Sabbath, and they say that day shall be kept holy, and around it they throw the safeguards of law, and they say that no man shall work on that day, unless it is a work that is absolutely necessary and cannot be foregone. . . . I cannot conceive how that a man who claims to be a peaceable, law-abiding citizen can go on disregarding the day openly in the face of law, openly in the face of protections that are thrown around the holy Sabbath, *as we believe it and hold it*, and protected by the laws of this State; and this is a question that I presume you gentlemen will not have any difficulty in coming to a decision upon." . . .

The State's attorney was correct in his statement to the jury that it was a question that he presumed they would "not have any difficulty in coming to a decision upon," as the jury in none of the four cases remained out over twelve minutes before returning a verdict of "guilty." (One case was dismissed for lack of evidence.)

On refusing to pay their fines, these four men were lodged in jail, June 3, where they remained from forty-five to fifty-three days each. The sheriff, Mr. Blackmore, a kind-hearted man, was loth to take them to jail, and remarked to the judge that the convicted were conscientious in the matter, to which the judge replied, "Let them educate their consciences by the laws of Tennessee." This statement is strangely out of harmony with the Constitution which the judge is sworn to uphold, which says, "No human authority can in any case whatever control or interfere with the rights of conscience," and that "no preference shall ever be given by law to any religious establishment or mode of worship."

Their reasons for going to jail in preference to paying fines and costs, are stated in the following extract from a letter received by the secretary of the National Religious Liberty Association at Chicago, from J. H. Dortch, one of the defendants:—

"We did not pay our fines and costs, which accounted to about twenty-five dollars each, because we considered them unjust; and besides, if we had paid them and returned to our work, we would have been re-arrested, and thus compelled to spend all the little property we own in paying fines."

The prisoners were allowed twenty-five cents a day for each day's imprisonment, in payment of fines and costs. Not satisfied with this punishment, the prosecution, after a diligent search among obsolete statues and decisions, finally arrived at the conclusion that the county jail was the county work-house, and consequently, on the morning of July 18, three of them were marched through the streets of Paris in company with three colored criminals, and compelled to labor at shoveling on the streets.

The chain-gang was composed of three honest, sober, industrious

Christian farmers, "good citizens," whose only crime (?) was that of doing farm labor on the first day of the week; and three negroes (sic.), whose crimes were drunkenness, discharging of fire-arms on the streets, fighting, and shooting at the city marshal. Strangely contrasted companions for a chain-gang! Three punished for their obedience to the commandment of God which reads, "Remember the Sabbath day to keep it holy. *Six days shalt thou labor* and do all they work, but *the seventh day is the Sabbath* of the Lord thy God;" and three for violations of the commandments of God in committing crimes against the persons of their fellow-men. And what at first would seem the strangest feature of this shameful persecution, is the fact that those most interested in it are professed followers of Jesus Christ,—followers of him who never attempted to force his teachings upon anyone, but who rebuked his disciples for desiring to do so. Yet to him who has studied the past, this is but the repetition of history; and there is little difference between the spirit which associated these Christian men with common criminals in the chain-gang, and the spirit which associated Christ with murderers, and crucified him with two malefactors.

Another proof that this is religious persecution, directed against the observance of the seventh-day Sabbath, is the fact that violations of the Sunday law on the part of others are passed unnoticed. While these four men were under confinement, the *Post-Intelligencer*, the official paper of Henry county, contained the following announcement of a Sunday excursion from Paris to Hollow Rock:—

"On Sunday next there will be a basket picnic at Hollow Rock. The P.T. & A. Ry. will give an excursion rate of fifty cents for the round trip from Paris. The train leaves Paris at 9:45 A.M., and returning, leaves Hollow Rock at 5:00 P.M."

The train carrying these Sunday picnicers passed within less than one hundred feet[166] of the cell containing the four Seventh-day Adventists in prison for quiet farm work done on Sunday. A letter dated "Paris Jail, Paris. Tenn., July 15," written by J. Moon, one of the imprisoned men, to his brother, Allen Moon, Washington,

D.C., presents the same fact, *i.e,*, that these parties are victims of an odious discrimination in the matter of enforcing the Sunday law, as the following extract from the letter will show:—

"While I am writing to you, it being Sunday, there is a trainload of workmen passing in the streets not thirty feet[167] from the jail, going out to work; and they have done so every Sunday since we have been here, and it apparently does not disturb any one. But if a poor Adventist takes his hoe out in his field and labors on Sunday, it disturbs the people for miles around."

Surely "justice standeth afar off, for truth is fallen in the streets, and equity cannot enter."

These cases are not the first convictions of the kind under the Tennessee statute. In 1886, W. H. Parker, another Seventh-day Adventist, spent seventy-four days in the same jail for Sunday work. At the same time James Stemm, one of the four men recently imprisoned, and William Dortch, father of the J. H. Dortch recently imprisoned, spent three months in the same jail for doing farm work on Sunday; and in 1890, R. M. King, of Obion county, whose case was carried to the United States Supreme Court, but suddenly terminated by the death of the defendant, was fined seventy-five dollars and costs by the same judge (Judge W. H. Swiggart) for performing his usual farm work on his own premises on Sunday. These persecutions, instead of destroying themselves by their own venom, have steadily increased in frequency and severity; and it now rests with the people of Tennessee to decide whether they will so adjust their laws as to make such persecutions impossible, or allow this outrage on the inalienable rights of God-fearing men and industrious citizens to go on.

A number of newspaper comments are appended, touching the cases referred to in the foregoing, to show that there is still a sentiment alive in this country in favor of religious liberty and opposed to such persecutions.

2

Newspaper Comments

It seems absolutely incredible that in this age of enlightenment, in these free United States, men should suffer and families be plunged into sorrow because they have exercised a right of conscience guaranteed to them by the Constitution of their country. The sooner a test case is appealed to the highest tribunal in the land for adjudication, the better for the honor of Tennessee and every State ridden by bad laws, passed in violation of individual liberty.—*Chicago Daily Globe*

There was no pretense, except in the indictment, that anybody had been at all disturbed by this secular employment. The peace was in no way threatened. No more was proven than that the Christian neighbors were scandalized that the law should be thus broken. And the great commonwealth of Tennessee has at its mercy some half-dozen patient, industrious, well-meaning citizens, religious beyond the ordinary practice of ordinary Christians, and so holds them because of an intolerance which, whatever may be the technical law, is opposed to the very spirit of our republican institutions.

There seems to be no remedy for it, and these men must serve out their sentences. But the sooner Tennessee places itself, through its Legislature, upon a par with liberal, right-minded people everywhere in the Republic, the better it will be for both the moral and the material prosperity of that State.—*Chicago Times*

Let us be careful how we let in the camel's nose of religious legislation, lest the brute crowd his bulky form in and occupy the whole shop. If the law by which these men were legally imprisoned be a righteous law, then may any State, nation, or country set up a religious creed and enforce it; then France treated properly the Huguenots; Russia the Jews, and early New England and Virginia the Baptists and Quakers. Protestant America had better be careful how she lays foundations for other men to build upon. Rome has as good a right to build in her way as we have in our way.—*Church Bulletin (Baptist), South Chicago*

It seems that Mr. King, who is a farmer, was indicted for quietly working on his own premises, "not in sight of any place of public worship." He disturbed no one by his work, but it was held that "the moral sense" of the people had sustained a shock by seeing work done on the Sabbath, and this statement was made against him at his trial.

But this is not all. The man was first carried before a Justice of the Peace; his case was heard, and the Justice imposed a fine of three dollars and costs, amounting in all to about twelve dollars. For the same offense he was afterward indicted by the Grand Jury, and fined the sum of seventy-five dollars.

The peculiar sect to which Mr. King belongs, observes Saturday as the Sabbath; hence the fact of his working on the first day of the week, and thereby offending the high moral sense of the good people in his neighborhood; and it seems that there is an association in Tennessee which is pledged to the prosecution of all violators of the Sunday laws of the State, and this unfortunate man has fallen under the ban of its displeasure.

He is evidently traveling in hard lines . . . . Whatever the merits of the case may be, Mr. King can count on public sympathy, for from the statement of it in the Tennessee papers, he appears to be a sadly persecuted man, and the history of the case thus far smacks of injustice and religious intolerance which is novel in its Puritanic severity. The man appears to have been dragged from court to court and jury to jury, subjected to great pecuniary expense, fined twice for the same offense—if an act like his, committed in accordance with the rules of his sect, can indeed be called an offense.—*Atlanta Constitution*

The keeper of Saturday has an undoubted moral right to his convictions. More than this, his legal right to observe Saturday as a holy day and Sunday as a secular day ought not to be called in question in free America, by any civil authority. It would not be in doubt for a moment were it not for the existence of legal anachronisms that should have gone out with the witchcraft laws, or at the latest, with George the Third.—*Boston Daily Globe*

It is not to be contended that Mr. King disturbed any neighbor in the employment of a quiet Sunday, but merely that this working on Sunday and his observance of Saturday as his Sabbath instead, was an offense to the moral sense of the community, and a violation of the laws of the State.

If it was so, it is high time for the community in which Mr. King lives, to discipline its moral sense, and for his State to re-arrange its laws in conformity with that principal of individual liberty which lies at the foundation of American institutions.

The principle involved is simple, and its application plain. The State has nothing to do with religion, except to protect every citizen in his religious liberty. It has no more right to prescribe the religious observance of Sabbaths and holy days, than to order sacraments and to ordain creeds.—*New York World*

So long as the labor of Adventists on Sunday does not interfere with the rights of the Mosaic and Puritanic people on the same day, the prosecution of them seems neither more nor less than persecution.—*Chicago Tribune*

People are asking if we are returning to the days of Cotton Mather or the Spanish Inquisition, that faithful, law-abiding citizens must be fined or driven from the country when their only offense consists in quietly carrying out the convictions of conscience. —*Louisville Courier Journal*

Mr. King is an honest, hard-working farmer. He is charged with no breach of morals, in fact it appears that he is a remarkably upright man; but he is a Seventh-day Adventist; that is, he does not hold the same religious views as the majority of his State. He stands in the same relation to his countrymen as that occupied by the early disciples of Christ to Roman society when Nero undertook to punish Christians by kindling nightly human fires for the delectation of conservative or majority thought. He is in the minority, even as the Huguenots were in the minority when the Church tortured, racked, and burned them for the glory of God and the good of humanity. He is in the minority as was Roger Williams when, in 1635, the popular and conservative thought of Salem banished him. Mr. King is not an infidel or even a doubter. On the contrary he is ardently religious, being a zealous member of a sect of Christians noted for their piety and faith . . . . In vain the long-cherished idea that this country was to pass down the cycle of time, known as the land of freedom; that it was to be forever the asylum of religious liberty and the cradle of progress, unless the sober thought of our people be at once aroused to stem the rising tide of governmentalism and the steady encroachment of religious organizations and despotic foreign thought. —*The Arena*

There can be but one opinion upon this decision among all liberal-minded men. It is odious sophistry ! unworthy of the age in which we live, and under it an American citizen has been condemned to spend the rest of his days in a dungeon, unless he shall stoop to deny the dictates of his own conscience, and dishonor his own manhood. —*New York Commercial Advertiser*

In all America there is not a class of people more law-abiding or God-fearing than are these Seventh-day Adventists, and it will be passing strange if they are not permitted to trace their religious belief back to the Fountain-head, and exercise the privilege of observing the original Sabbath, so long as they are not interfering with the rights of others.—***Spokane Falls Review***

Not being able to leave his crops unworked for two days in the week, Mr. King plowed them on Sunday after having kept the Sabbath the day before. He was arrested under the Sunday law, and in order to make it effective against him, it was alleged that his work on his own farm on Sunday created a public nuisance. On this entirely untenable ground, he has been harassed from court to court. He was a poor man, but has been supported by the friends of religious liberty. Mr. King has been greatly wronged, but his only remedy at law is under the law and constitution of Tennessee. It appears that for the present his remedy is denied him, and this being the case, he has no better course than to submit to the oppression and go to prison—to the convict camp, if it suits the convenience of his persecutors to send him there.—***St. Louis Republic***

All these religious laws and prosecutions which have stained the history of the Church in all ages, come not from an earnest, Christian desire to elevate mankind, but from the malicious disposition of the professor of religion to punish the man who dares to question the superior excellence of his professions. The religious Sunday observer of Tennessee could afford to be lenient with the squirrel hunters whose rifles could be heard popping in the timber on all hours of that holy day. He could easily ignore their violations of his Sunday law because the transgressors were low white trash whose influence cut no figure. But when a man making equally high religious professions with himself, whose life was just as pure and exemplary, who derived the authority for his position from the same sacred volume from which he derived his, and could defend his position with arguments and citations which could not be refuted,—when such a man disputed the sanctity of his Sunday observance, a challenge was thrown out which he could not afford to ignore without serious sacrifice of his professed sanctity. It was not Mr. King's immortal soul he cared to save from the consequences of his Sunday labor; it was Mr. King's influence that challenged the soundness of his theology, and set at naught his assumed religious superiority and authority, and aroused a combative malice that would have lighted the fagots around the seventh-day observer, had the law of the State permitted it. —*Sigourney (Iowa) Review*

The law which does not allow a man who rests on Saturday to work on Sunday, in such a way as not to interfere with the rest of others, is bad law and bad morals and bad religion.—*New York Independent*

If in any State the Adventist, the Hebrews, or any other people who believe in observing Saturday instead of Sunday, should happen to predominate, and they undertook to throw Christians into dungeons, and after branding them criminals, should send them to the penitentiary for working on Saturday, indignation would blaze forth throughout Christendom against the great injustice, the wrong against the liberty of the rights of the citizen. The only difference is that poor Mr. King is in the minority; he is the type of those who always have been, and always will be, made to suffer when the government is strong enough to persecute all who do not accept when is considered truth and right by the majority. —*The Arena—In the Chain-Gang for Conscience' Sake*, **National Religious Liberty Association [1892], pp. 1-11.**

Endnotes

1   Alexander Proudfit, D. D., "The Duty of Parents to Their Children, A Discourse Based On Proverbs 22:6."

2   During the years that Miller was a deist, he enjoyed entertaining his deist friends by mimicking the piety of his Baptist relatives.

3   The "son" mentioned here was Erving G. Guilford, a nephew of William Miller, being the son of Miller's younger sister, Sylvia (Miller) Guilford, and her husband, Silas Guilford.

4   About 25 km.

5   The printed article from which this is copied was written in 1845. By an examination of his [Miller's] correspondence, it appears that he must have begun to lecture in August, 1831. So this date is a mistake of the printer or an error in Mr. Miller's memory. As no mention is made of this in the letter to Elder Hendrix, from which the previous extract is made [not quoted here], he could not have gone to Dresden before the second Sabbath [i.e. Sunday] in August, 1831 [i.e. August 14, 1831].

6   According to notes kept by William Miller in his "Text Book," he used Titus 2:13 to open more series of meetings than any other Bible text.

7   On February 6, 1844, Bates sold his home in Fairhaven, Massachusetts, to Noah Spooner for $4550.

8   Heman S. Gurney (1817-1896).

9   Charles Fitch was one of two men that Ellen Harmon-White, in her first vision, was shown will be in Heaven. See *Early Writings*, p. 17.

10   Charles Fitch died in Buffalo, New York, on Monday, October 14, 1844 (just eight days prior to when he expected the Lord to return on October 22.)

11   This refers to the preceding pages in Sylvester Bliss's *Memoirs of William Miller*, from which this quotation is taken.

12   Himes was then living in Elk Point, South Dakota.

13   1844.

14   The Stowell family lived in Paris, Maine.

[15]   Oswald Stowell

[16]   Prudence (Nye) Bates died August 27, 1870, at her home in Monterey, Michigan. She was 77 years old.

[17]   Owen R. L. Crosier (1820-1913).

[18]   Dr. Franklin B. Hahn (1809-1866).

[19]   Esther (Marier Persons) Edson (1816-1893). Esther was Hiram Edson's second wife, having married him in 1839.

[20]   Most likely it was *The Day-Star "Extra"* of February 7, 1846.

[21]   Heman S. Gurney (1817-1896).

[22]   Robert Harmon, Sr. (1786-1866).

[23]   James White (1821-1881).

[24]   Apparently Heman Gurney either had forgotten, or was unaware of the fact, that Ellen G. Harmon's first two times in print were letters that she had written to Enoch Jacobs of Cincinnati, Ohio. Her letters had appeared in the January 24, 1846, and February 27, 1846, issues of Jacobs' paper, *The Day-Star.*

[25]   Actually, Gurney could not have become a "Seventh-day Adventist" in 1845, as the name was not chosen until 1860. But he did become a Sabbath-keeper that year, and would later become a Seventh-day Adventist.

[26]   1.6 km.

[27]   Ellen Harmon (later White) was 17 when Gurney first heard her speak.

[28]   Sarah Harmon (1822-1868). She later married Stephen Belden. One of their children was the Adventist hymn writer, F. E. Belden.

[29]   The trip here referred to is the one he took in early 1844 with Joseph Bates from Fairhaven, Massachusetts, where they both lived, down into Maryland. See p. 14.

[30]   Joseph Bates' first tract on the Sabbath.

[31]   Located across the Acushnet River from Fairhaven in New Bedford, Massachusetts.

[32]   Mr. Benjamin Lindsey.

[33]   Joseph Bates (1792-1872).

[34]   Sarah Harmon (1822-1868). She later married Stephen Belden.

[35]   Province of Ontario since 1867.

[36]   The original Washington hand press was destroyed when the Review and

Herald Publishing Company building in Battle Creek, Michigan, burned to the ground on the night of December 30, 1902.

[37]   All three of these are in western New York State.

[38]   Silver three-cent coins were minted in the United States from 1851 to 1873.

[39]   Mary Loughborough (1832-1867).

[40]   New York.

[41]   New York.

[42]   11.2 km.

[43]   .8 km.

[44]   64 km.

[45]   Esther Edson (1816-1893).

[46]   Train.

[47]   Merritt E. Cornell (1827-1893).

[48]   At the time the *Present Truth* was started in 1849, James and Ellen White were living in the attic of Albert Belden's home in Rocky Hill, Connecticut.

[49]   January 14, 1857.

[50]   Sunday. Rather than referring to the days of the week by their pagan names, our early Sabbath-keeping Adventist pioneers simply called them "First-day," "Second-day," etc., except for the seventh day, which was always called "Sabbath."

[51]   9.6 to 16 km.

[52]   -34.4 degrees celsius.

[53]   Joseph Bates was sixty-five years old at the time he performed this baptism at Monterey, Michigan.

[54]   Rather than staying in Colorado, later in that year, 1859, Merritt G. Kellogg and his family went on to California, thus, as far as is known, becoming the first Sabbath-keeping Adventists in that state.

[55]   Nebraska.

[56]   Nebraska.

[57]   1.6 km.

[58]   7.6 cm.

59   12.7 cm.

60   1.52 m.

61   1.83 m.

62   .4 km.

63   About 12.8 to 16.1 km.

64   22:30.

65   80 km.

66   Aspinwall, Panama, on the eastern coast of Panama.

67   Panama City, Panama, on the western coast of Panama.

68   John Loughborough and the Bourdeaus left Battle Creek June 8, 1868. They spent two weeks at Rochester, New York, purchasing a tent and supplies for their journey. While in Rochester, John was united in marriage to Margaret A. Newman, his first wife having died in 1867. Elder Bourdeau performed the ceremony.

69   1.6 km.

70   9600 km.

71   96 km.

72   Her family in 1874 consisted of her parents, Alonzo L. and Stella Baker, and her maternal grandmother.

73   Mrs. McKibbin had a very light skin complexion.

74   She was referring to a painting of the Yountville camp meeting. There are no known original photographs of the Yountville camp meeting.

75   Presses for minting gold bullion into coins.

76   At the time of this 1967 interview, Mrs. McKibbin was a member of the Mountain View, California, Seventh-day Adventist church.

77   17:00.

78   Mary Andrews was the daughter of Elder John N. and Angeline Stevens Andrews.

79   Not so. Mary Andrews is buried in Mt. Hope Cemetery in Rochester, New York, next to her mother and sister, Carrie, who had preceded her in death.

80   112.6 km.

81   16.1 to 56.3 km.

82   40.2 km.

83   80.5 km.

84   40.2 km.

85   L. Dyo Chambers and his wife lived in Chattanooga, Tennessee. He was secretary of the Tract Society located there.

86   1.63 hectares.

87   32.2 km.

88   120.8 km.

89   9.7 km.

90   Marion E. Cady (1866-1948); president of Healdsburg College, Healdsburg, California (1899-1903).

91   Healdsburg College, the forerunner of Pacific Union College, operated from 1882 to 1908. Starting as an academy, it was elevated to a college. The school was located in Healdsburg, California.

92   1.6 km.

93   1865-1955.

94   Ida May (Bauer) Magan (1869-1904).

95   1865-1952.

96   1860-1951.

97   48.3 to 128.7 km.

98   1858-1935.

99   Elder Spicer was reelected General Conference president in 1926; he finally was able to retire from that office in 1930.

100   James and Ellen White lived in Rochester, New York, from 1852 to 1855.

101   Presumably the five cent coins were silver half dimes, since no nickels were minted until 1866.

102   Construction of an office building for the Pacific Press Publishing Co. that was in the process of being established in Oakland, California.

103   24.4 x 33 m.

104   20.1 x 7.9 m.

105   14 x 7.9 m.

106   At the camp meeting held in October, 1874, at Yountville in Northern California, donations and pledges totaling $19,414 were given toward the

establishment of the new Pacific Press Publishing Co. that was soon to be organized in Oakland, California.

[107]   Obviously this footnote in Robinson's book is in error, since the year is wrong.

[108]   Obviously this footnote in Robinson's book is in error, since the year is wrong.

[109]   At that time approximately $300.

[110]   At that time approximately 25 cents.

[111]   At that time approximately $25.00.

[112]   Ellen White's oldest grandchild, Ella M. (White) Robinson, 1882-1977.

[113]   Ellen White's home in Australia from 1896 to 1900. It was located near Avondale College in Cooranbong, New South Wales.

[114]   Ellen White's second oldest grandchild, Mabel White (Workman), 1886-1981.

[115]   In Vicksburg, Mississippi.

[116]   6.1 x 12.2 m.

[117]   Dan Stephenson was a native of Mississippi. He was the teacher at the new little Adventist school when it opened in Calmar, Mississippi, in early 1899.

[118]   James Edson White, 1849-1928, the second son of James and Ellen White.

[119]   William H. Casey was superintendent of the 800-acre Bruce Plantation. He accepted the Sabbath in 1898.

[120]   N. W. Olvin was a sharecropper on the 800-acre Bruce Plantation. He accepted the Sabbath in 1898.

[121]   N. W. Olvin.

[122]   F. R. Rogers and his wife, Minnie, and their small son, Chester, arrived in Yazoo City, Mississippi, from Walla Walla, Washington, in November, 1898. Rogers spent the next fourteen years ministering to blacks until, broken in health by too many malarious summers, he went to Michigan to die.

[123]   1898.

[124]   1899.

[125]   6.4 km.

[126]   Elder Arthur G. Daniells, 1858-1935.

[127]   607 hectares.

[128]   At that time approximately $3.50.

[129] At that time approximately $75.00.

[130] Elder Stephen McCullagh.

[131] At that time approximately $5,000.

[132] At that time approximately $2,500.

[133] At that time approximately $1,500.

[134] Because of the British way of writing dates, the date was April 5, 1899.

[135] When I was a student at La Sierra College in the 1960's, I heard Elder Arthur L. White in a classroom guest lecture tell this story—he had heard Elder A. G. Daniells tell it. Elder White said that the banker had gold coins stacked all over the counter counting them for the bank audit the next day —James Nix.

[136] At that time approximately $375.

[137] At that time approximately $2,000.

[138] At that time approximately $500.

[139] At that time approximately $1,000.

[140] At that time approximately $1,500.

[141] In a vision given to Ellen White on Christmas Day, December 25, 1865, in Rochester, New York, she was shown that Seventh-day Adventists should establish our own health institute.

[142] The General Conference session at which Ellen White related her vision calling for the establishment of an Adventist health institution opened on May 16, 1866, in Battle Creek, Michigan.

[143] Elder John N. Loughborough, 1832-1924.

[144] Father of Dr. J. H. Kellogg and W. K. Kellogg, who are credited with being the inventors of corn flakes.

[145] Dr. Horatio S. Lay, 1828-1900.

[146] Dr. Phoebe Lamson, fl. 1860's.

[147] Ellen G. White, *Life Sketches*, 1915, p. 403

[148] Ellen G. White, Letter 153, 1902.

[149] 30.76 hectares.

[150] 6.4 km.

[151] 12.5 hectares.

[152] 8.9 hectares.

[153]   1.6 km.

[154]   *Medical Evangelistic Library*, No. 4, p. 25.

[155]   Minutes of Southern California Conference, June 20, 1905.

[156]   At that time the Southern California Conference included most of the territory now included in both the Southern and Southeastern California Conferences.

[157]   This meeting was held in the Carr Street church in Los Angeles.

[158]   The purchase price of $40,000 originally included the following terms: The owners wanted $20,000 on or before January 1, 1906. Payments were $1,000 down to secure the property until June 13, 1905; $4,000 more due on June 15; another $5,000 due by the last of July; another $5,000 due the last of August; with the remaining $5,000 due on or before January 1, 1906. The final $20,000 was to be secured by a mortgage on the property for three years.

[159]   Elder G. W. Reaser, president 1905-1908.

[160]   This was the payment that was due the last of July, 1905.

[161]   At that time the California Conference contained most of the territory now included in the Central and Northern California Conferences.

[162]   Later he is referred to as J. W. Lewis; which is correct is unknown to the compiler.

[163]   This bracketed comment is in the original pamphlet.

[164]   This bracketed comment is in the original pamphlet.

[165]   Earlier he was referred to as A. W. Lewis; which is correct is unknown to the compiler.

[166]   30.5 m.

[167]   9.1 m.

References

Joseph Bates, *Autobiography of Joseph Bates* (Steam Press of the Seventh-day Adventist Publishing Association, 1868)

Joseph Bates, *Second Advent Way Marks and High Heaps* (Press of Benjamin Lindsey, 1847)

Joseph Bates, "Letter from Brother Bates," *The Advent Review and Sabbath Herald* (February 19, 1857)

Joseph Bates, "The Review and Herald," (January 13, 1852)

Henry B. Bear, *Henry B. Bear's Advent Experience* (unknown date)

Sylvester Bliss, *Memoirs of William Miller* (Published by Joshua V. Himes, 1853)

Luther Boutelle, *Sketch of the Life and Religious Experience of Elder Luther Bautelle* (Advent Christian Publication Society, 1891)

Ms. Boyd, "The First Italian Tract," *The Advent Review and Sabbath Herald* (September 18, 1924)

"Brother Charles Fitch," *The Midnight Cry* (October 31, 1844)

George I. Butler, *Review and Herald* (August 16, 1881)

John O. Corliss, "The Message and Its Friends-No. 5, John N. Andrews, Its Pioneer Missionary," *The Advent Review and Sabbath Herald* (September 6, 1923)

Mrs. M. C. Stowell Crawford, "A Letter from a Veteran Worker," *The Watchman* (April 25, 1905)

Mrs. V. O. Cross, "Recollections of the Message," *The Advent and Sabbath Herald* (April 1, 1920) vol. 97, Nos. 14, 22

Heiram Edson and F. B. Hahn, *The Day-Star,* "Extra" (February 7, 1846)

General Conference Daily Bulletin (October 29, 1889, Volume 3, Number 9)

Paul A. Gordon and James R. Nix, *Laughter and Tears of the Pioneers* (North America Division Office of Education, 1989)

Paul A. Gordon, *Herald of the Midnight Cry* (Pacific Press Publishing Association, 1990)

Ronald D. Graybill, *Mission to Black America* (Pacific Press Publishing Association, 1971)

H. S. Gurney, "Gurney Statement Re 'To the Remnant," (May 15, 1891)

H. S. Gurney, "Recollections of Early Advent Experience," *The Review and Herald* (January 3, 1888)

Merritt G. Kellogg, M. D., *Notes Concerning the Kellogg's* (1927)

Anna Knight, *Mississippi Girl* (Southern Publishing Association, 1952)

Richard B. Lewis, *Streams of Light, The Story of the Pacific Press* (Pacific Press, 1958)

John N. Loughborough, "Sketches of the Past-No. 74," *Pacific Union Recorder* (July 29, 1909)

John N. Loughborough, "Sketches of the Past-No. 143," *Pacific Union Recorder* (February 12, 1914)

John N. Loughborough, "Sketches of the Past-No. 75," *Pacific Union Recorder* (August 12, 1909)

John N. Loughborough, "Second Advent Experience-No. 7," *The Advent Review and Sabbath Herald* (July 26, 1923)

John N. Loughborough, "Second Advent Experience-No. 4," *The Advent Review and Sabbath Herald* (June 28, 1923) 9-10

John N. Loughborough, "Sketches of the Past-No. 139," *Pacific Union Recorder* (June 19, 1913)

John N. Loughborough, "Sketches of the Past-No. 144," *Pacific Union Recorder* (March 19, 1914)

John N. Loughborough, "Sketches of the Past-No. 140," *Pacific Union Recorder* (July 3, 1913)

John N. Loughborough, "Sketches of the Past-No. 142," *Pacific Union Recorder* (November 27, 1913)

John N. Loughborough, "Sketches of the Past-No. 141," *Pacific Union Recorder* (October 30, 1913)

John N. Loughborogh, "Reminiscences of the Life of Uriah Smith," *Advent Review and Sabbath Herald* (April 7, 1903)

John N. Loughborough, *Rise and Progress of the Seventh-day Adventists* (General Conference Association, 1892)

Harold O. McCumber, *Pioneering the Message in the Golden West* (Pacific Press Publishing Association, 1946)

J. L. McElhany, "Life Sketch of Elder J. O. Corliss," *The Advent and Sabbath Herald* (October 25, 1923)

Alma E. McKibbin, *Step By Step* (Review & Herald Publishing Association, 1964)

William Miller, *Apology and Defence* (Pamphlet Published by J. V. Himes, 1845)

Washington Morse, "Items of Advent Experience During the Past Fifty Years-No. 6," *Advent Review and Sabbath Herald* (November 6, 1888)

James R. Nix, "The Life and Work of Hiram Edson," (unpublished term paper, 1971)

M. Ellsworth Olsen, *Origin and Progress of Seventh-day Adventists* (Review & Herald Publishing Association, 1932, 3rd edition)

Portland Tribune (October 12, 1844)

Mrs. L. B. Priddy, "A Bit of Church History," *The Advent Review and Sabbath Herald* (September 18, 1924)

Dores E. Robinson, *The Story of Our Health Message* (Southern Publishing Association, 1965, 3rd edition revised)

Ella M. Robinson, *S. N. Haskell, Man of Action* (Review & Herald Publishing Association, 1967)

Virgil Robinson, *James White* (Review & Herald Publishing Association, 1976)

Virgil Robinson, *Flame for the Lord* (Review & Herald Publishing Association, 1975)

Richard A. Schaefer, *Legacy Daring to Care* (Legacy Publishing Association, 1995)

Richard W. Schwarz, *John Harvey Kellogg, M.D.* (Southern Publishing Association, 1970)

Uriah Smith, "History and Future Work of Seventh-day Adventists," (Sermon, Sabbath, October 26, 1889)

Arthur W. Spalding, *Origin and History of Seventh-day Adventist* (Review & Herald Publishing Association, 1962, vol. 1)

Arthur W. Spalding, *Footprints of the Pioneers* (Review & Herald Publishing Association, 1947)

Arthur W. Spalding, *Pioneers Stories of the Second Advent Message* (Southern Publishing Association, 1942 revised edition)

Jean Vuileumier, "The Last Days of Elder J. N. Andrews," *Review and Herald* (September 18, 1924)

Jean Vuilleumier, "Early Days of the Message in Europe-No. 4," *Review and Herald* (April 18, 1929)

Ellen G. White, *Testimonies for the Church, No. 32* (Pacific Press Publishing Association and Review & Herald Publishing Association, 1885)

Ellen G. White, *Selected Messages* (Review & Herald Publishing Association, 1958, bk. 1)

Ellen G. White, *Life Sketches* (Pacific Press Publishing Association, 1915)

James White, *Review and Herald* (June 8, 1869)

James White, *Life Incidents* (Steam Press of the Seventh-day Adventist Publishing Association, 1868)

B. L. Whitney, "Death of Elder J. N. Andrews," *The Review and Herald* (November 20, 1883)

Index of Stories